Writer/Designer

A Guide to Making Multimodal Projects

Writer/Designer

A Guide to Making Multimodal Projects

Second Edition

Cheryl E. Ball
West Virginia University

Jennifer Sheppard
San Diego State University

Kristin L. Arola
Michigan State University

bedford/st.martin's
Macmillan Learning
Boston | New York

For Bedford/St. Martin's

Vice President, Editorial, Macmillan Learning Humanities: Edwin Hill
Senior Program Director for English: Leasa Burton
Program Manager: Molly Parke
Marketing Manager: Vivian Garcia
Director of Content Development: Jane Knetzger
Developmental Editor: Leah Rang
Associate Content Project Manager: Matt Glazer
Workflow Manager: Lisa McDowell
Production Supervisor: Robert Cherry
Assistant Editor: Stephanie Cohen
Editorial Services: Lumina Datamatics, Inc.
Composition: Lumina Datamatics, Inc.
Photo Editor: Angela Boehler
Photo Researcher: Lumina Datamatics, Inc.
Director of Rights and Permissions: Hilary Newman
Senior Art Director: Anna Palchik
Text Design: Claire Seng-Niemoeller
Cover Design: John Callahan
Cover Images: pika111/Getty Images
Printing and Binding: RR Donnelley

Printed in China.

2   1   0   9   8
f   e   d   c   b

For information, write: Bedford/St. Martin's, 75 Arlington Street, Boston, MA 02116

ISBN 978-1-319-05856-2 (Student Edition)
ISBN 978-1-319-10779-6 (Instructor's Edition)

Acknowledgments

Art acknowledgments and copyrights appear on the same page as the art selections they cover; these acknowledgments and copyrights constitute an extension of the copyright page.

At the time of publication all Internet URLs published in this text were found to accurately link to their intended website. If you do find a broken link, please forward the information to writerdesigner@macmillan.com so that it can be corrected for the next printing.

Preface for Instructors

We know that creating multimodal projects and assignments can seem daunting and bring up a lot of questions for both students and instructors. What's the best way to get students started with a multimodal project? Is it necessary to learn a lot of new technologies? How do you introduce multimodal activities into the writing classroom, even if the final project is text-based? How do you assess multimodal work? In this second edition of *Writer/Designer*, we aim to help you answer these questions and more, making multimodal composing strategies and projects even more accessible to you and your students. We know how to help you through it because we've been there—throughout the book, you'll be learning from the successes, mistakes, and experiences we've had teaching, supervising, and creating multimodal work in classes ranging from first-year writing to advanced media courses.

The title of this book, *Writer/Designer: A Guide to Making Multimodal Projects*, reflects our belief that writing and designing always work together. Whether authors are working with words, images, sound, or movement, decisions about what content says and how it looks and functions are necessarily entwined, even when we don't pay conscious attention to their relationship. We want our students to always be aware of how writing and designing work together, to think of themselves as equal parts writers and designers. Both design and content influence how audiences respond to a text's message, so developing familiarity with design concepts and practices as well as textual and rhetorical composition is critical for successful communication. This book helps students to develop these skills together, providing them with a rhetorical toolkit for making purposeful, relevant, and persuasive choices in their writing and designing.

The concepts of design and process that we introduce in this book provide a foundation for any composition course and a guide for any instructor looking to incorporate multimodality, no matter your experience or expertise with media or technologies. For this second edition, we listened to feedback from composition instructors—program administrators, professors, grad students, and part-time faculty—teaching in two-year schools and four-year schools, online courses and cinder-block-walled classrooms to make *Writer/Designer* even more flexible and accommodating to different course objectives and instructors' varying levels of comfort with teaching multimodality. New Touchpoint activities showcase ideas for multimodal practice through learning key writing and design concepts, and these can be used independently as in-class work. Larger Write/Design! assignments are more detailed to lend you support and guidance, and a new Write/Design! Option added to the chapter-ending assignments presents ways to incorporate multimodality into core writing assignments, such as literacy narratives and rhetorical analyses. With these revisions, plus new examples of real student work and authentic Case Studies, the second edition of *Writer/Designer* increases its commitment to support instructors' and students' teaching and learning of the multimodal composing process in creative and engaging ways.

We know from our own professional experiences and those of colleagues who share our pedagogical interests that integrating multimodal projects into our teaching can often lead to feeling like we are "ambassadors of multimodality" for our students, programs, and departments. Each of us has experienced the need to justify the significance of our multimodal pedagogies and what they offer to students preparing for academic and professional life. Although the focus of *Writer/Designer* is on helping students develop compositional and rhetorical strategies, we also provide explanations of multimodality's value that will be of use to instructors who need to make the case that facility with diverse literacies and modalities will strengthen students' rhetorical and communicative skills. The book's clear, accessible guidance for teaching multimodal composition may help ambassadors discuss multimodal pedagogy with writing program administrators, department heads, colleagues, and teaching assistants.

Further rationales on the value and significance of multimodality can be found in an annotated bibliography, presented as part of the Instructor's Manual.

Multimodality, Genres, and Life

Whether at school, on the job, or just in everyday life, multimodal texts have become an essential part of communication in nearly every arena of contemporary culture. The widespread use of design and media software, Web technologies, and other digital media has increased opportunities to convey information and has also changed the expectations of readers. We wrote this book specifically to help authors learn how to make conscious multimodal choices in the texts they create, no matter what mode, medium, or rhetorical situation they are working in. With the guidance and activities we've provided in *Writer/Designer*, authors—your students—will be more prepared for the complex rhetorical challenges they face as students and future professionals.

We designed this book to support the integration of multimodal projects into classrooms through both short-term and semester-long projects. The book offers accessible strategies for composing with multiple modes of communication, including detailed examples and explanations of what multimodality means, definitions and examples of key design concepts, rationales for why multimodality matters, and in-depth support for composing multimodal projects within a variety of contexts and technologies. The chapters use a mix of student-produced and real-world projects to illustrate the rhetorical choices and strategies discussed.

We organized this second edition to lead authors through a chronological process in analyzing, planning, and designing multimodal texts in Part One and to apply specific strategies and tools from the Toolkit in Part Two, according to the affordances and needs of their particular projects and processes. In addition to this flexible structure, we also kept it brief enough to meet any instructor's individual needs and personal expertise. The assignments we've included can support authors in creating their own projects in any genre or situation. Our original inspiration for the book came from talking with colleagues in fields as diverse as business, political science, and geology about the kinds of multimodal texts they asked their students to produce, and about how those processes could be supported using the rhetorical methods we were trained to teach within our own writing classes. *Writer/Designer* is meant to be easy to use in any number of courses across disciplines, either on its own or bundled with your favorite textbook or handbook. The Instructor's Manual includes sample syllabi to demonstrate how *Writer/Designer* can be used in a variety of courses, as well as tips and strategies for using the activities in your course.

Grounded in Theory, Supported in Practice

This book is grounded in our own praxes, pedagogies, and theoretical leanings. We are particularly influenced by the New London Group (NLG)—a group of literacy scholars who make the deceptively simple argument that "literacy pedagogy must now account for the burgeoning variety of text forms associated with information and multimedia technologies." Their work makes the case that such pedagogies more richly prepare students for the diverse rhetorical and communicative practices they need to succeed as students, as professionals, and as citizens in the twenty-first century.

As friends in graduate school in the early 2000s, we were immersed in the NLG's pedagogy of multiliteracies when it was used by our writing program faculty to reimagine the first-year writing course we all taught. Rather than concentrating exclusively on written text, we were introduced to a model of composition instruction that focused on integrating written, oral, and visual communication. This curriculum helped students learn to craft texts in a variety of modes and genres to best meet their diverse rhetorical needs.

In the years since our first experiences in that multimodal classroom, we've gone on to specialize in different areas of rhetoric and writing studies, but the theory and pedagogy of what we experienced in those early days continue to influence our work today. Cheryl's work as editor of the journal *Kairos* helps the field of writing studies rethink how scholarship about digital writing can be modeled in digital, multimodal forms; Jenny regularly teaches courses in visual and professional communication and digital and popular culture rhetorics, and she publishes on the intersection of theory and practice in digital writing, multimodal composing, professional communication, and pedagogy; and Kristin's work brings together composition theory, digital rhetoric, and American Indian rhetorics so as to understand digital composing practices within larger social and cultural contexts. As we've developed and refined syllabi in a variety of courses, created our own multimodal projects, and mentored authors through their composition processes, we've discovered a series of best practices, backed up by theory, that we want to share with you. This book benefits from our collective experiences and builds from many of the assignments and syllabi we've designed, as well as from the editorial process Cheryl uses in *Kairos*. You can see some of these syllabi and other curricular materials in the Instructor's Manual.

One of the biggest lessons we've learned is the value of learning-by-doing through writing for authentic audiences and purposes (what the New London Group would call "situated practice"). Incorporating multimodal composition projects into the classroom provides valuable avenues for students to explore all available means of persuasion for communicating their ideas in any rhetorical situation. Learning to communicate persuasively requires sustained opportunities to practice this kind of composition, in addition to an awareness of general rhetorical strategies and the affordances offered by different media and modalities. Providing students with the chance to experiment and reflect on composing in different modalities will help them develop the confidence and competence they need to leverage both old and new technologies and media for successful communication.

Additionally, the examples and processes discussed in this book draw from both classroom and real-world texts to help students see how multimodality works in a variety of contexts and genres. We provide tools for critically analyzing available resources, as well as for understanding how different modes can be brought together in creative and complex ways to convey new meanings across multiple, new situations. Research in rhetorical genre studies suggests that this method of recursive analysis and production, specifically done within genres that are found in everyday life, helps authors learn how to write in multiple situations. The Instructor's Manual offers an annotated bibliography that covers issues of rhetorical genre studies, multiliteracies, multimodal composition, and more.

Features of the Book

- **A process-focused approach** introduces and illustrates key stages of multimodal composition while establishing clear connections to the writing process and to the practices students will actually use in creating their projects.

- **A central emphasis on design** introduces and illustrates foundational concepts of design—*contrast, organization, alignment, proximity*, and more—to provide students the tools they need to develop multimodal texts.

- **Write/Design! Assignments** in every Part One chapter help students dig into chapter concepts and scaffold students' development of larger-scale projects. They ask students to complete assignments such as a genre conventions analysis for their chosen project, a proposal for developing and delivering their multimodal projects, and a report on the final project or draft. **Write/Design! Options** offer assignment options in classes where asking students to complete a large-scale, semester-long project may not be desirable. They ask students to complete activities such as a multimodal literacy narrative, rhetorical analysis of several multimodal texts of their choosing, and a genre analysis of visual arguments.

- **Touchpoint** activities (formerly called Process! activities) throughout each chapter prepare authors to apply multimodal concepts from the book to small-stakes practice—either sample multimedia texts and scenarios (in Part One) or their own projects (in Part Two). Touchpoint activities teach students about practices such as examining modal affordances, analyzing project designs, learning about fair use and different kinds of Creative Commons licenses, developing practices for successful collaboration, and creating drafts of their projects through rapid prototyping techniques.

- **Case Studies** highlight and analyze actual (published or presented) examples of multimodal texts. In Case Studies, we provide in-depth analyses of an author's composing processes that correspond to the stage of writing/designing outlined in that chapter. Case Studies also showcase how the design vocabulary or concepts we present in each chapter are put into practice in the design process. Example texts from Case Studies include a rhetorical and design analysis of a university website, a student team's pitch for an interactive museum app, and two designers' revision process for a journal advertisement.

Whether you are new to teaching multimodal projects or someone who has lots of experience, we designed this book to give your students a strong foundation in the concepts and practices of multimodal composing. You'll also find the additional materials in the Instructor's Manual helpful. In it, we've compiled more assignments, syllabi, and supporting content to provide further ideas on integrating multimodality into your writing classes.

New to This Edition

From the outset, *Writer/Designer* was meant to be an attractive, accessible, and highly readable guide to multimodal composition—a brief book that made a new, complex process easier. The second edition is even more committed to those goals. With new examples of multimodal texts, more detailed standalone activities for in the classroom and out, and updated design coverage, *Writer/Designer* is now more flexible and useful for student writer/designers.

- **Expanded coverage of essential design and rhetorical concepts** in Part One chapters give authors a stronger foundation for multimodal composing. Examples and analysis of design terms such as *color*, formerly found in *ix: visualizing composition*, are now incorporated directly into the book, and new sections on multimodal genres and technology strategies provide writer/designers support to create their own projects.

- **A more flexible Write/Design! assignment** now offers options for each project: an immersive multimodal and multimedia process or a more streamlined approach that allows students to incorporate multimodal elements into core assignments such as literacy narratives or rhetorical analyses.

- **More hands-on practice with Touchpoint activities**, which suggest small-scale, small-stakes assignments that let authors learn by doing. Touchpoints work as standalone multimodal activities to practice rhetorical concepts or as scaffolding support for ongoing multimodal projects.

- **A new organization** provides structure for students and instructors during the multimodal process.

  - **Part One: The Processes of Writing and Designing** (Chapters 1–5) introduces key concepts of multimodality, rhetoric, genre, process, and peer review while allowing authors to practice applying their new knowledge with examples, activities, and assignment projects.

  - **Part Two: The Write/Design Toolkit** (Chapters 6–7) offers a flexible collection of strategies and activities for multimodal processes that can be assigned alongside the Part One chapters and with a wide range of projects. Sections include Working with Multimodal Sources; Copyright Issues and Ethics; Organizing and Sharing Assets; Assessing Technological Affordances; and Drafting Your Project: Static, Dynamic, and Timeline-Based Texts, which offers in-depth examples for designing project drafts that include sketches, mock-ups, storyboards, and rough cuts, depending on students' needs.

- **Updated examples and images** pique students' interest, showcase real-world write/design situations, and keep *Writer/Designer* relevant. New visuals include protest imagery from the Black Lives Matter movement, a "re-gendered" girls' magazine cover, roller-derby posters, and mobile apps.

Acknowledgments

This book would never have been possible without the guidance and support of the people we worked with over the years at Bedford/St. Martin's. For their early inspiration for this book, we'd like to thank Joan Feinberg and Denise Wydra. We would also like to thank Edwin Hill, Vice President of Macmillan Learning Humanities Editorial; Molly Parke, Program Manager for Rhetorics and Business and Technical Communication; and Leasa Burton, Senior Program Director for English, for helping us think through different iterations of this project since 2004. Leasa's kind editorial mentorship helped us to conceptualize (and reconceptualize) our project from initial proposal to finished product. We also offer our gratitude to Leah Rang, development editor, for her guidance through re-envisioning the second edition. Her insight, attention to detail, and unending patience ensured that this book would be relevant, timely, and (to Cheryl's continued delight) full of lolcats. A special thanks to Lucy Johnson, Washington State University, for tackling the updates to the Instructor's Manual for this edition.

We'd also like to recognize the many other people at Bedford who contributed to this book: Matt Glazer, associate content project manager, for his patience and attention to detail; Stephanie Cohen, assistant editor, for any number of behind-the-scenes tasks; Paula Bonilla, copy editor; John Callahan, cover designer; Vivian Garcia, marketing manager, for working to get the word out about the book; Hilary Newman, director of permissions, and Richard Fox, art researcher; and Jake Kawatski, indexer, for his careful attention to themes and subjects. Thank you, thank you, thank you.

Thanks are also due to the following reviewers for their invaluable feedback in focus groups, over phone calls, and on early drafts of our manuscript: Shawn Apostel, Bellarmine University; Margaret Arballo, California State University, Sacramento; Tim Bang, St. Cloud State University; Jeremy Benson, Rhode Island College; Benjamin Bishop, Des Moines Area Community College; Brenta Blevins, University of North Carolina at Greensboro; Emily Bouza, University of Mary Hardin–Baylor; Deborah Breen, Boston University; Cynthia Brewer, Austin Community College; Nicholas Brown, Texas Christian University; Rebekah Buchanan, Western Illinois University; Hugh Burns, Texas Woman's University; Jimmy Butts, Louisiana State University; Lanette Cadle, Missouri State University; Carolyn Calhoon-Dillahunt, Yakima Valley Community College; Amy Camp, College of DuPage; Jeaneen S. Canfield, Oklahoma State University; Dànielle Nicole DeVoss, Michigan State University; Virginia Dow, Liberty University; Matt Felumlee, Heartland Community College; Morgan Gresham, University of South Florida; Jennifer Hewerdine, Southern Illinois University; Karyn Hollis, Villanova University; Laura Howard, Kennesaw State University; Adam Kaiserman, College of the Canyons; Jason Kahler, Saginaw Valley State University; Elizabeth Kleinfeld, Metropolitan State University of Denver; Julian Knox, University of South Alabama; Heather Lang, Florida State University; Candice van Loveren Geis, Northern Kentucky University; Cat

Mahaffey, University of North Carolina Charlotte; Lucy Manley, Valley Forge Military College; Monica Miller, Georgia Institute of Technology; Lilian Mina, Auburn University at Montgomery; Amy Nejezchleb, Bellevue University; Jill Parrott, Eastern Kentucky University; Lisa Phillips, Illinois State University; Talinn Phillips, Ohio University; Kris Purzycki, University of Wisconsin–Milwaukee; Mark Putnam, University of Northwestern Ohio; Susan Rauch, Texas Tech University; Kristin Ravel, University of Wisconsin–Milwaukee; Jim Ridolfo, University of Kentucky; Bill Riley, Rose-Hulman Institute of Technology; Meg Ruggiero, Appalachian State University; Katie Sagal, Heartland Community College; Robin Snead, University of North Carolina at Pembroke; Sarah Summers, Rose-Hulman Institute of Technology; Gina Szabady, Lane Community College; Jenna Vinson, University of Massachusetts Lowell; Tammy Winner, University of North Alabama; and Zhiwei Wu, Guangdong University of Foreign Studies. Their insights helped us to focus our approach and to keep the needs of a diverse instructor and student population in mind as we wrote.

Finally, we'd like to say a special thanks to the people in our immediate lives who have supported our work on this project. We are grateful to our many students and friends who allowed us to use examples of their work to help others learn. These samples would not have been possible without their graciousness.

Cheryl would like to thank the multiple dozens of people she has learned from and been inspired by since this book first came to fruition—too many to name without fear of missing one, but the editorial staff and many authors she has worked with at *Kairos* deserve a shout-out for helping her think through this curriculum in real-world settings over the past few years. In addition, Cheryl expresses deep thanks to Sarah Lowe (and her students) and Lydia Welker for allowing her to share their in-progress work so that others may learn from it in the Case Studies. Cheryl is also grateful for her colleagues at West Virginia University, who make Morgantown a productive and thoughtful place to live and work, as well as her colleagues and students at the Oslo School of Architecture and Design, from whom she has gleaned much design knowledge over the last four years. Thank you. And, finally, a huge hug to Kristin and Jenny for putting up with her, still.

Jenny would like to extend her thanks to her partner, Kathryn, who graciously took on extra childcare and household duties while she worked on the book. Her overall support and willingness to talk through ideas were instrumental in the project's completion. Jenny would also like to thank Cody Archer, Edgar Barrantes, Edreanne "Anna" Calaycay, CC Chamberlin, Paul Jensen, Phillip Johnson, Alicía Leon, Joyce Melendez, Cory Moore, Sarah Tanori, Alejandra Villavicencio, and Hannah Willis for their permission to reproduce several of the examples used in the book, as well as the many students with whom she has worked over the years. She has learned an immeasurable amount about multimodal composing from their efforts and experiences.

Kristin would also like to thank her amazing colleagues and graduate students at Washington State University. Watching Dr. Patricia Ericsson gracefully integrate multimodality into a first-year composition course, and then seeing talented instructors like Amy Petersilie creatively and critically engage with a multimodal pedagogy, has been an invaluable and awe-inspiring experience. Thanks to all of her past undergraduate students who make her job worth doing, especially those who gave permission for their work to be used in this book—Huizi Li, Nicole Schmidt, Courteney Dowd, Ariel Popp, Nicholas Winters, and Elyse Canfield—and extra special thanks to Lucy Johnson for always helping her think critically about how to best teach and engage with multimodality. Thanks to those family members, friends, and friends of friends who graciously share their artistic talents with the world, and allowed her to share a piece of that in this book—Elena Duff, Adam Arola, Leigh Feldman, and Tom O'Toole. And finally, thanks to Jeff, who continues to feed her heart, soul, and belly with all things good.

We're all in. As always.

Bedford/St. Martin's is as passionately committed to the discipline of English as ever, working hard to provide support and services that make it easier for you to teach your course your way.

Find **community support** at the Bedford/St. Martin's English Community (community.macmillan.com), where you can follow our *Bits* blog for new teaching ideas, download titles from our professional resource series, and review projects in the pipeline.

Choose **curriculum solutions** that offer flexible custom options, combining our carefully developed print and digital resources, acclaimed works from Macmillan's trade imprints, and your own course or program materials to provide the exact resources your students need.

Rely on **outstanding service** from your Bedford/St. Martin's sales representative and editorial team. Contact us or visit macmillanlearning.com to learn more about any of the options below.

Choose from Alternative Formats of *Writer/Designer*

Bedford/St. Martin's offers a range of formats. Choose what works best for you and your students:

- *Spiral-bound*   To order the flexible spiral-bound edition, use ISBN 978-1-319-05856-2.

- *Popular e-book formats*   For details of our e-book partners, visit **macmillanlearning.com/ebooks**.

Select Value Packages

Add value to your text by packaging any Bedford/St. Martin's resource, such as Writer's Help 2.0, with *Writer/Designer* at a significant discount.

Writer's Help 2.0 is a powerful online writing resource that helps students find answers, whether they are searching for writing advice on their own or as part of an assignment.

- **Smart search.** Built on research with more than 1,600 student writers, the smart search in Writer's Help provides reliable results even when students use novice terms, such as *flow* and *unstuck*.

- **Trusted content from our best-selling handbooks.** Choose *Writer's Help 2.0, Hacker Version,* or *Writer's Help 2.0, Lunsford Version,* and ensure that students have clear advice and examples for all of their writing questions.

- **Diagnostics that help establish a baseline for instruction.** Assign diagnostics to identify areas of strength and areas for improvement and to help students plan a course of study. Use visual reports to track performance by topic, class, and student as well as improvement over time.

- **Adaptive exercises that engage students.** Writer's Help 2.0 includes LearningCurve, game-like online quizzing that adapts to what students already know and helps them focus on what they need to learn.

Student access is packaged with *Writer/Designer* at a significant discount. Order ISBN 978-1-319-16730-1 for *Writer's Help 2.0, Hacker Version,* or ISBN 978-1-319-16743-1 for *Writer's Help 2.0, Lunsford Version,* to ensure your students have easy access to online writing support. Students who rent or buy a used book can purchase access and instructors may request free access at **macmillanlearning .com/writershelp2**.

Instructor Resources

You have a lot to do in your course. We want to make it easy for you to find the support you need—and get it quickly.

Instructor's Manual for Writer/Designer is available as a PDF that can be downloaded from macmillanlearning.com. Visit the instructor resources tab for *Writer/Designer*. In addition to chapter overviews and a list of key concepts and skills, the instructor's manual includes sample syllabi, correlations to the Council of Writing Program Administrators' Outcomes Statement, classroom activities and assignments for multimodal composing, and suggestions for how to use each chapter in class.

Contents

2 How Does Rhetoric Work in Multimodal Projects? 34

3 Why Is Genre Important in Multimodal Projects? 60

4 How Do You Start a Multimodal Project?   86

5 How Do You Design and Revise with Multiple Audiences?   111

PART TWO   The Write/Design Toolkit

6 Working with Multimodal Assets and Sources 147

Introduction for Students

Although the three of us are trained as writing teachers, we have always been interested in new media and nontextual means of communicating. Don't get us wrong; we love words, and we love helping people learn how to craft them. Writing will continue to be important for a long time to come. However, we've also come to see that elements beyond words can be just as effective—or more so!—in conveying a message. Our goal in this book is to help you take advantage of every possibility that's out there—not just words but also sound, images, movement, and more—so you can create communications that perfectly meet your goals, your situation, and the needs of your audience.

We often ask our students to create texts of all kinds, and we decided to write this book as a way to support writers in that complex and sometimes messy process. As writers, designers, and communicators who for many years have worked on creating interactive digital projects, video presentations, websites, social networking profiles, new media journals, online courses, and more, we are interested in conveying information and ideas using the most appropriate means and media at our disposal. Through this book, you'll learn from the successes we've had and the mistakes we've made as teachers and authors.

Notice we just said "authors" here, but elsewhere in this book we'll refer to the people who produce content as "designers," "writers," and "communicators." You might be saying that writers don't design, or that communicators don't write. We don't believe that's true (and that's why we called this book *Writer/Designer*). Using a multimodal approach to reading or composing a text, you'll start to recognize that *all* writing is designed, even if it doesn't look like much thought was put into those one-inch margins. And the converse is usually true as well, in that most designs involve some kind of writing. We believe that communication comes in many forms and that it is all created with some deliberate attention to writing and design. It may not be a kind of writing that you recognize or that you think would "count" as acceptable writing in a professional setting such as school or work, but as this book will show you, even something as seemingly simple as a text message can be carefully written and designed.

At this point in your life, you've likely come to realize that good writing doesn't just happen. You're probably familiar with the idea that writing is a process, with various stages required to get to a final product. Similarly, good multimodal projects don't just happen—they involve planning, researching, drafting, and revising. Although these stages may look a little different for each writer and each project, being able to draw on this basic process can help you create texts that will be complete and persuasive to your intended audience. This book will help you hone a composing process that works for you, no matter what kind of project you are creating.

Just as important, this book will provide you with a toolkit for analyzing and creating texts in many modes and for many different audiences. Although we'll talk a lot about digital texts, we'll provide ideas for nondigital texts, too. Also, this isn't a how-to book about specific technologies or software applications. We'll give you guidance on how to think through the *who*, *what*, *why*, and *how* of your projects so that you can use whichever communication mode, genre, or technology will best suit your audience and purpose. You'll find that this approach is more beneficial in the long run because you'll be able to apply these practices to whatever new technology emerges next.

Features of the Book and How to Use Them

We spent a lot of time thinking about how to design this book to support the variety of projects you might take on. We've worked to provide clear explanations and lots of examples, particularly in the Case Studies, to help illustrate the concepts and practices we talk about. We have included short Touchpoint activities throughout each chapter so that you can get some quick experience putting concepts into practice. We've also included longer Write/Design! assignments (with options) in each chapter in Part One to guide you through the steps of creating larger-scale projects. We have used many of these activities and assignments with our own students to help them develop ideas, design projects, and communicate through multiple modes.

Above all, as you use this book, we want you to keep in mind that creating multimodal projects can be a lot of fun. Yes, there are bound to be frustrations along the way as you work through the many possibilities, but your communication options are no longer limited to typing words in a twelve-point font on an 8.5" x 11" piece of paper. We invite you to dive in, experiment, and see what opportunities you have to convey your ideas, arguments, and information.

Writer/Designer

A Guide to Making Multimodal Projects

The Multimodal Process

What Are Multimodal Projects?

Academic essays, biology posters, PowerPoint presentations, memes . . . what do all these texts have in common? They are all **multimodal**.

The word *multimodal* is a mash-up of *multiple* and *mode*. A **mode** is a way of communicating, such as the words we're using to explain our ideas in this paragraph or the images we use throughout this book to illustrate various concepts. Multimodal describes how we combine multiple different ways of communicating in everyday life.

For instance, Internet memes such as lolcats, as well as many Instagram posts and Snapchats, are multimodal. Lolcats combine photographs of cats with Internet speak (words written in humorously incorrect grammar) to create a text that uses both visuals and language—*multiple modes*—to be funny.

You might be saying to yourself, "Wait, is a lolcat really a text?" Yes. ***Text*** traditionally means written words. But because we want to talk about the visuals, sounds, and movement that make up multi-media, we use the term *text* to refer to a piece of communication as a whole. A text can be anything from a lolcat to a concert tee shirt to a dictionary to a performance.

The following figures all depict multimodal texts:

Figure 1.1 Lolcat Meme

Michelle Tribe, https://www.flickr.com/photos /greencolander/4299692892/

Figure 1.2 A Website

© 2013 National Museum of Natural History, Smithsonian Institution

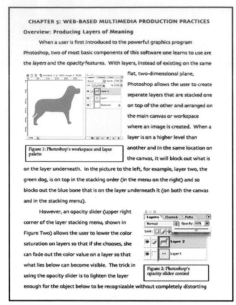

CHAPTER 5: WEB-BASED MULTIMEDIA PRODUCTION PRACTICES

Overview: Producing Layers of Meaning

When a user is first introduced to the powerful graphics program Photoshop, two of most basic components of this software one learns to use are the *layers* and the *opacity* features. With layers, instead of existing on the same flat, two-dimensional plane, Photoshop allows the user to create separate layers that are stacked one on top of the other and arranged on the main canvas or workspace where an image is created. When a layer is on a higher level than another and in the same location on the canvas, it will block out what is on the layer underneath. In the picture to the left, for example, layer two, the green dog, is on top in the stacking order (in the menu on the right) and so blocks out the blue bone that is on the layer underneath it (on both the canvas and in the stacking menu).

Figure 1: Photoshop's workspace and layer palette

However, an opacity slider (upper right corner of the layer stacking menu, shown in Figure Two) allows the user to lower the color saturation on layers so that if she chooses, she can fade out the color value on a layer so that what lies below can become visible. The trick in using the opacity slider is to lighten the layer enough for the object below to be recognizable without completely distorting

Figure 2: Photoshop's opacity slider control

Figure 1.3 A Dissertation

Figure 1.4 A Performance

Timothy J. Carroll, https://www.flickr.com/photos/tjc/5763847134

What Is Multimodal Composing?

Writers choose modes of communication for every text they create. For example, the author of a lolcat chooses the cat photo (usually based on what is happening in the photo and whether that action might make for a good caption) and decides where to place the caption and what color and typeface to use. Sometimes these choices are unconscious, like when an author uses Microsoft Word's default typeface and margins when writing a paper for class. Sometimes those choices are made explicitly by an author, and that's when **design** becomes purposeful. To produce a successful text, writer/designers must be able to consciously use different modes both alone and in combination to communicate their ideas to others.

A text does not have to include bright colors or interesting videos to be multimodal (although it can). Even a research paper, which is mostly words, is a multimodal text. Let's take **Figure 1.3** as an example. It might seem that an audience could understand this text's argument just by reading the written words. In fact, to understand the full message being communicated in the text, the audience has to make sense of other elements as well. They must also look at the images and read the captions that explain what the images contain. Even the font choice is an important but often subtle visual signal to the audience. (Are you using a font that screams traditionalism like Times New

Roman or one that invokes levity and youth, such as Comic Sans?) The format of the text—a single column of black printed words on a white background, with a margin on either side—also tells the audience something important: this text is probably an academic work of some kind. (In fact, it's a page from Jenny's dissertation.) Knowing what kind of text it is will influence the way the audience reads it.

Why Should Multimodal Composing Matter to You?

Multimodal projects are fun! But they're not *just* fun. They're useful and flexible and timely—just as writing is—while also doing double or triple the communicative work of writing due to the multiple layers of meaning that the modes of communication carry.

Take, for example, **Figure 1.5**. Artist Katherine Young was unhappy with the way girls' magazines portrayed their needs and goals in a way that only emphasized fashion and friends. The original cover of *Girls' Life* uses color, font size, and capitalization to draw readers' attention to the magazine's features, all related to appearance or relationships: fashion, kisses, "dream" hair, and "Wake up pretty!" An arrow and curved line just under the title connects the cover model with what the magazine deems valuable: her style. Young redesigned this magazine cover to emphasize girls' needs and goals

Figure 1.5 The Original *Girls' Life* Cover (left) and Young's Redesign (right)

involving career, health, and community. By reusing an existing design for the teen magazine genre and making smart choices for text, font, color, image, and layout, Young made a multimodal feminist statement—without needing to explicitly state the issue or her stance.

In the world, in your everyday life, texts are never monomodal, never *just* written, but are always designed with multiple media, modes of communication, and methods of distribution in mind. Learning how to analyze and compose multimodal texts prepares you for that kind of writing—the kind you will use every day of your life. Whether you work from home, in a large corporation, in a small nonprofit organization, or in some other professional or personal setting, you *will* need to write. And writing in the twenty-first century is always multimodal.

This whole book is about the *what* and *how* of multimodal composition, but the *why* is the motivation for it. We draw inspiration from a group of multimodal communication scholars (called the New London Group) who explain the *why* this way: Multimodal composition allows us to become **makers of our social futures**. That sounds exciting, doesn't it? But what exactly does it mean? By learning to compose multimodal texts instead of rehashing the limited use of written essays, writer/designers can communicate in more globally aware, digitally driven, ethical, and accessible ways, making our society a better place. The magazine cover redesign in **Figure 1.5** is a great example of using multimodality to (re)make our social futures.

Research-based writing typical of academic essays is important, but it's only one part of learning how to write. Authors need to be flexible and draw on any possible way to communicate that might be effective. In that way, the fundamental goals of writing and designing are the same:

- To think critically about the kinds of communication that are needed in any given situation
- To choose sources and assets that will help create an effective text
- To work within and fulfill your audience's needs and goals
- To improve communication through the finished text
- To create change or encourage positive action through a text

While these aims for multimodality might seem grandiose if you're just learning how to design a text, they can be implemented in even the smallest ways. Using an image speaks volumes towards a designer's goal of being globally, ethically, and accessibly aware through multimodality. There are more than seven billion people in the world

Figure 1.6 Using Images for Social Justice

A woman stands in front of an advancing police barricade during a Black Lives Matter protest. How does the image convey meaning differently than written text could?

Jonathan Bachman/Reuters/Newscom

and thousands of languages. But writing and designing through multimodality, with visuals that are more universal, can help us be mindful in how we represent or collaborate with those who are not exactly like us. Multimodal texts, such as the photograph in **Figure 1.6**, can be shared or used ethically to promote social and racial justice and remind us that we are all on this planet together.

All the examples used in this book are meant to provoke discussion as to how texts work through the media and modes they use. Sometimes the way a text works is unexpected and funny, such as a parody, but texts can also be hateful and mean-spirited. (Don't worry: We won't be showing any hateful texts in this book!) One of our goals is to help you understand that every text has an audience, but you might not always be a willing audience member. There may be images in this book that you don't like—such as the lolcat on the first page that two authors of this book dislike (Jenny and Kristin are dog people). But it behooves you to think critically about how such texts are made and how they make meaning so that you can (1) listen to and appreciate the perspective of others and (2) learn how to make your own multimodal arguments for the good of all. This book helps you do that, whether you're a student, a teacher, an entrepreneur, a mom, a Snapchat fanatic, or all of the above.

Writing/Designing as a Process

Whenever an author begins writing a text, it is always a **process**, even if that process has become so implicit through practice that the author no longer recognizes the multiple steps she may take to complete a text. She begins from scratch, thinking about what she needs to say and the way she needs to say it to communicate to her audience. (This part of the writing process is called *analyzing the rhetorical situation*, which we will discuss in Chapter 2.)

The Typical Writing Process

Writing a research paper doesn't begin with the moment of inscription—putting words on a page. A lot of thinking, talking, brainstorming, and research needs to be done before a topic can even be settled on. But once an author has begun drafting a paper, it will probably go through multiple rounds of writing and revision, particularly if it is a high-stakes project like a research paper, thesis, or business report. For instance, drafting might involve preliminary research on the audience, topic, and delivery method required (such as types of sources or citation systems needed). This work is often done to prepare for writing, but when a paper draft is due, the author might work more closely to format the report with the correct spacing, grammar, punctuation, citation styles, and so on. Any necessary revisions require the author to revisit the drafting and formatting stages before presenting the final text to the audience. This writing process is called *recursive* because writers interact with audiences at several parts of the process, get oral or written feedback from sample audiences or stakeholders, and revise—this is a typical process enacted in writing classes.

The Multimodal Composing Process

When we write texts that are more overtly multimodal than a research paper, we use the same recursive process just outlined: different levels of drafting, revising, and more fine-tuned drafting until we only need to polish the final text. Just as authors choose from available words and genres to create their new texts, designers choose from existing examples and assets, working recursively to create a new multimodal text suitable for a new audience. **Figure 1.7** shows how this recursive process works in design. Designers get feedback from audiences just like writers do to help them create better and more effective multimodal texts. (This feedback process will be described in more detail in Chapter 5.)

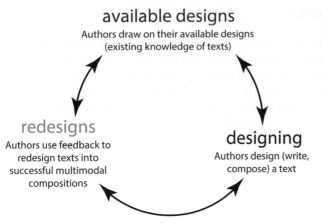

available designs

Authors draw on their available designs
(existing knowledge of texts)

redesigns

Authors use feedback to
redesign texts into
successful multimodal
compositions

designing

Authors design (write,
compose) a text

Figure 1.7 The
**Recursive Writing and
Design Process**

The user feedback loop is
discussed more in Chapter
4 (pp. 94–95).

During the design process, multimodal texts may take several different forms. Although some people assume multimodal texts always have to be digital, that's not actually true. A multimodal text may be designed using digital methods (such as a word processor), a mixture of digital and analog methods (such as note cards to draft a PowerPoint presentation), or may be totally analog (such as a pen-and-ink drawing or collage). All these design decisions are based on what the audience needs during the drafting and feedback process and what modes and media will suit those needs from drafts to final product. For instance, the dissertation in **Figure 1.3** was created on a computer but then was printed and bound into a book for the library. No matter whether a text is created on a computer, on paper, or in some other medium or technology, writer/designers can still use the multiple combinations of words, photos, color, layout, and more to communicate their information.

Sometimes designers pick the wrong medium and have to start over from scratch with the "inscription" part of the process. Although writing-heavy texts can be more easily revised using cut-and-paste methods, more heavily multimodal texts that combine audio, visuals, and other modes of communication can be more challenging to revise. Each mode of communication and each medium used in a multimodal text necessitates a new layer of revision. That's one reason why the multimodal composing process often involves different forms at different stages of the process. Starting with a storyboard with paper and stick figures to lay out a short film, for example, makes it easier to make a pitch to investors or quickly (and cheaply) change a sequence; revising a recorded and edited film with visuals, audio, and text overlay is much more complex and better suited to later stages of the process.

Touchpoints

Touchpoints are important to the design process for multimodal projects because they are how designers pinpoint, assess, reflect, and redesign all the different steps in a situation or text as the potential audience will encounter it. The term *touchpoint* comes from the discipline of design, where it refers to ephemeral or real points of interaction between stakeholders (users, service providers, etc.) in a designed experience. Points of interaction vary depending on the kind of experience designers are working with.

For example, one kind of experience might be a tourist using an interactive map on her phone. Touchpoints in that experience could include an app store with information on downloading the map, the tourist's surroundings as she is downloading the app, her phone connectivity source (data or wireless), the map interface and how she interacts with it, the way directions are stored (offline or online only) as she begins her trek, and so on. There are hundreds of touchpoints possible in a single experience, and touchpoints ensure that designers understand the full scope of work they need to create to effectively reach their audience and fulfill a particular need.

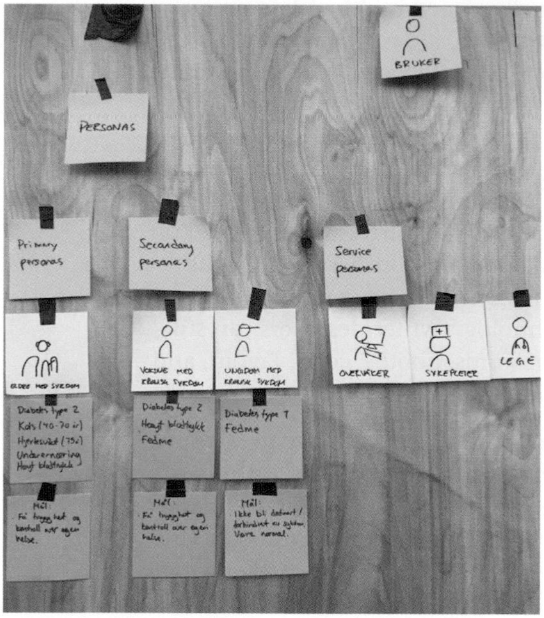

Assessing touchpoints can be a large or small endeavor, depending on the size of the multimodal project. In one major study, a team of designers at a university hospital in Norway evaluated and mapped the dozens of touchpoints (and waiting times) that a breast cancer patient needed to engage with, from her first appointment with a general practitioner to her diagnosis, and then redesigned the four-month process down to a four-day process. The sticky notes in **Figure 1.8** represent

Figure 1.8 Touchpoints for a Medical App

Quick sketches on sticky notes depict different audiences (user groups, or personas) for a medical app. In yellow from left to right: the infirmed elderly, adults and adolescents with chronic illnesses, and the service personnel (technicians, nurses, and doctors) who interact with the Web app.

Photo by Cheryl Ball with permission of Hans-Martin Erlandsen a small portion of the touchpoints for a customer-service journey through a hospital rehabilitation Web service. This example, created by Norwegian design student Hans-Martin Erlandsen, represents a half-meter (approximately 1.5 feet) section of a wall in a larger mapping of touchpoints that spans a 3-meter (roughly 10-foot) wall space, all covered with various sticky notes, printouts from a medical website prototype, clippings of articles, and arrows that label and point to important parts of the interaction process that need redesigning.

We introduce the concept of touchpoints here because we will use it throughout the book to assess your understanding of making multimodal projects—either through a short analytical exercise (such as the one that follows) or through application to your own project.

◎— Touchpoint: **Understanding Multimodal Processes**

Imagine describing all the points of interaction that an airline passenger must encounter to book a ticket, get to the airport, go through security, find her gate, board the plane, and upon arrival, disembark, find her baggage, and so on. (If you've never flown before, a bus or train service can be substituted, or some other mode of transportation.) How would you redesign such an experience to make it easier and more enjoyable for that passenger, from start to finish? Consider how an app might work: from booking to using the same app at the gate to board, then using the app to map your location in the new airport and get directions to the correct baggage carousel. How would that app work regardless of your user's ability, race, creed, color, religion, orientation, or other social or cultural status? Are they a non-native English speaker? Blind? In a wheelchair? Deaf? Elderly? Transgender? A parent with a toddler? Traveling with pets? These questions help designers think about how multimodal projects can reach audiences both similar to and unlike themselves:

- How would touchpoints be different for each set of these potential users?

- Which touchpoint would be the first to create a diversion from the suggested route for any one of these groups of users?

- How would the app be designed to accommodate *all* of these potential users? What elements might you incorporate that go beyond written text? How should it operate?

Consider how touchpoints might work in your own writing and designing projects as you move through this book.

How Does Multimodality Work?

All kinds of texts are multimodal: newspapers, science reports, advertisements, billboards, scrapbooks, music videos—the list is endless. Consider, for example, all of the modes at play in a simple TV commercial—there usually is music, the voice of an announcer, video showing the product, text on the screen giving you a price or a Web address, and often much more. Each of these modes plays a role in the advertiser's argument for why you should buy its product. The music is selected to give the product a certain feel (young and hip, perhaps, or safe and reliable). The gender of the announcer and the tone, volume, and other qualities of his or her (or their) voice reflect whom the advertiser is trying to reach. The choice of whether to use video or animation, color or black and white, slow motion or other special effects, are all deliberate *modal* considerations based on what the advertiser is trying to sell and to whom. Although each mode plays a role in the overall message, it is the combination of modes—the *multi*modality—that creates the full piece of communication.

To help you think through the different modes that may be present in a multimodal text, we're going to introduce you to five terms from the work of the New London Group, a collection of education and literacy scholars who first promoted the concept of multimodal literacies. They outlined five modes of communication—linguistic, visual, aural, gestural, and spatial—which they found could be applied to any kind of element in a text.

Every text is made up of individual **elements**. Elements in a text might include specific words or phrases, colors, and individual images that are used—all of which audiences can read individually—to form an overall, cohesive meaning for the text. Although *element* doesn't seem much more specific than *thing*, it is the placement and relation of the elements in a text that offers meaning for the whole.

The photograph in **Figure 1.9** can be split into individual elements: the beach, the trash on the sand, the garbage can, and the sign on the side of the can. Each of these elements can be broken down and categorized to add up to one ironic whole. Although this is a static photo, it is also easy to imagine adding sound to this image. As an element within this multimodal composition, sound could play an important role in guiding our reading of a

Figure 1.9 Elements Combined to Create an Ironic Image

sdominick/Getty Images

text. If this photo were set to the sound of a cheering crowd, it would read differently than if it were accompanied by the sound of chirping birds. The next section will help you better understand how different elements use individual modes of communication to make meaning.

Linguistic Mode

The linguistic mode refers to the use of language, which usually means written or spoken words. When we think about the ways the linguistic mode is used to make or understand meaning, we can consider:

- word choice
- the delivery of text as spoken or written
- the organization of writing or speech into phrases, sentences, paragraphs, etc.
- the development and coherence of individual words and ideas

Figure 1.10 The Five Modes of Communication

This chart of the modes is based on a diagram created by the New London Group.

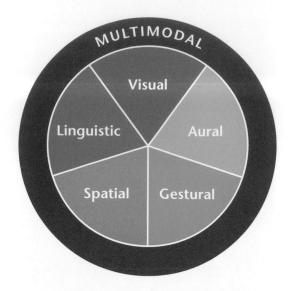

While these aren't the only possibilities for understanding how the linguistic mode works, this list gives you a starting place from which to consider how words and language function. And although we've listed it first—and although it's the mode you probably have the most practice with—the linguistic mode is not always the most important mode of communication. (Whether it is or not depends on what other modes are at play in a text, what kind of text it is, and many other factors.)

The linguistic mode and the ability to use it carefully matter very much in contemporary communication. For example, consider a widely criticized comment made by Carl-Henric Svanberg, chairman of the global oil company BP, following the 2010 oil spill in the Gulf of Mexico. After meeting with then-President Barack Obama, Svanberg announced that his company was committed to the cleanup and stated that BP "care[s] about the small people." Although he likely was referring to BP's commitment to helping individual citizens, his choice of words—"small people"—infuriated the public because it demeaned those impacted by the spill and implied that the disruption to their lives was not of great concern.

Visual Mode

The visual mode refers to the use of images and other characteristics that readers see. Billboards, flyers, television, websites, lighted advertising displays, and even grocery store shelves bombard us with visual information in an effort to attract our attention. We can use this mode to communicate representations of how something looks or how someone is feeling, to instruct, to persuade, and to entertain, among other things. The visual mode includes:

- color
- layout
- style
- size
- perspective
- framing

Many of the ways we can talk about the visual mode, such as color and size, seem fairly straightforward, but perspective and framing might need a bit more definition here. **Framing** positions a viewer to see a visual text from a certain perspective and offers a way to describe how a visual text is presented—both its literal frame, like a window or picture frame (the lines around what we see), and the sight lines within it that draw our focus. Focusing on how something is framed helps us think about what is important in a text.

If you look at the photo "Self in Waiting" in **Figure 1.11**, you will see several different frames that serve to group elements, direct the viewer's attention, and otherwise communicate the photographer's purpose. The woman's arm in the foreground creates a horizontal frame with the bottom of the windowsill, thus emphasizing what we see above this line. The left edge of the windowsill creates a vertical frame, with the woman on the left side and the window on the right. The woman's left arm is a diagonal line against the vertical and horizontal lines of the window and her right arm. Where these three lines come together (the horizontal, the vertical, and the diagonal) we see the telling position of her right wrist, and a focal point of the image. What might the location of this focal point indicate to viewers, gesturally? Spatially? (Read more in the following sections to find out about these and other modes.)

Figure 1.11 "Self in Waiting"
© Mandie Rose Danielski

For low-vision and blind audiences, the visual mode will often be replaced by aural or spatial modes. For instance, screen-reading programs that convert written text such as transcripts, captions, or website navigation to speech are an important technology to consider when designing a multimodal text. Versions of texts in Braille, a tactile writing system, may also be made available in print using a Braille typewriter or through a refreshable Braille display that reads text on screens and displays the tiny bumps of Braille on an external mechanical device for audiences to feel (see **Fig. 1.12**). These aural and spatio-gestural versions of texts are useful tools to help the low-vision reader make meaning of texts, and some of these options can also help other readers who may desire or require transcripts to parse visual texts.

Figure 1.12 **Braille Keyboard with a Refreshable Braille Display**

zlikovec/Shutterstock

Aural Mode

The aural mode focuses on sound. Whether we are talking about a speech, a video demonstration, sound effects on a website, or the audio elements of a radio program, the aural mode provides multiple ways of communicating and understanding a message, including:

- music
- sound effects
- ambient noise/sounds
- silence
- tone of voice in spoken language
- volume of sound
- emphasis and accent

Although most of us are used to hearing sound all around us every day, we don't often pay attention to how it signals information, including feelings, responses, or needed actions. It's easy to conceive how a spoken message communicates, but what about the increasingly tense background music in a TV drama, or the sounds that let us know when a computer is starting up, or the tones our smartphones make when a text message comes in? Whether big or small, each of these aural components conveys meaning for hearing audiences, just as silence or the absence of sound does.

For deaf or hard-of-hearing audiences, other modes in the form of linguistic and visual information often replace aural information. For instance, closed captions (see **Fig. 1.14** on p. 18) that present dialogue and other aural information on screen-based texts help deaf audiences make meaning of those texts, and they can also be of use to unintended audiences, such as the elderly with hearing loss or, more cheekily, viewers watching their favorite news show on their phones during a meeting.

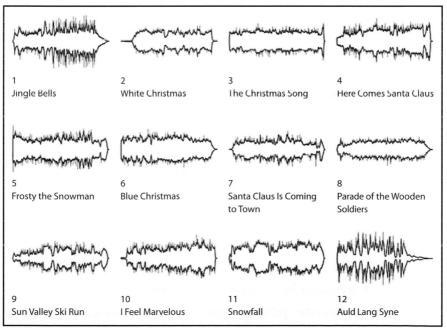

Figure 1.13 Graphic Comparison of Christmas Song Waveforms
Audio can also have visual aspects, as these representations show.

The most compelling thing that I've seen is a 7km wetland being reduced to nothing

Figure 1.14 Closed Captioning

This video was captured to showcase the work of a class of first-year and senior-level design students at Cape Peninsula University of Technology in Cape Town, South Africa, as they prepared a design project to study sustainability and climate change with the local community. The captions help visualize an off-screen narrator's voiceover.

Spatial Mode

The spatial mode is about physical arrangement. This can include how a brochure opens and the way it leads a reader through the text. For example, see the brochure in **Figure 1.15**. The designer created this conference program so that each fold is slightly smaller than the one below it, allowing readers to have a tab for each day of presentations. The spatial mode can also refer to the placement of navigation on a Web page to maximize access for users. This mode helps us to understand why physical spaces such as grocery stores or classrooms are arranged to encourage certain kinds of behavior (such as all chairs in a classroom facing toward the center of the room to encourage discussion and collaboration). The spatial mode includes:

- arrangement
- organization
- proximity between people or objects

Attention to the spatial mode has become increasingly important as we create content for and interact within online environments such as smartphones. The author of a text must pay attention to how his or her content is organized so that readers can find their way through it without difficulty.

Figure 1.15 Tabbed Brochure Utilizing the Spatial Mode
Edgar Barrantes

Gestural Mode

The gestural mode refers to the way movement, such as body language, can make meaning. When we interact with people in real life or watch them on-screen, we can tell a lot about how they are feeling and what they are trying to communicate. The gestural mode includes:

- facial expressions
- hand gestures
- body language
- interaction between people

The gestural has always been important in face-to-face conversations and in the theater, but understanding the gestural mode is just as important when communication takes place through virtual interactions on-screen. Whether we are participating in a video conference with colleagues, a gaming raid with friends, or an online chat with family, the gestural mode provides a way of connecting (or showing an inability to connect) to other people.

Gestures can even be interpreted in static images, such as in the 1930s posters in **Figure 1.16** (p. 20) from Franklin Delano Roosevelt's New Deal. Hundreds of posters were created to publicize health and safety, education, and community programs. The poster on the left has a strong horizontal split-frame that divides two statements, one that poses a problem and the other that suggests a solution. In the bottom half, a woman (presumably a teacher?) holds a piece of paper

Figure 1.16 New Deal Posters

Library of Congress, Prints & Photographs Division, Library of Congress, Prints & Photographs Division, Reproduction number LC-USZC2-5332 (color film copy slide) LC-USZCN4-205 (color film copy neg.); Library of Congress, Prints & Photographs Division, Reproduction number LC-USZC2-1116 (color film copy slide)

close to John's face, while John looks on with discomfort. (Likely, as the poster notes, because he needs glasses.) The body language of the two people helps visually tell the story. The poster on the right has a strong diagonal split from the top of the hammer down to the bright yellow piece of metal on the anvil, a yellow matched by the text. The framing here conveys a sense of directed purpose, immediacy, and action (a split second from now, that hammer will strike home).

Gestures convey a lot of emotion and meaning, as much if not more than words can, although writer/designers should remember that not all people in an audience might be able to move, gesture, or see those gestures in the same way. One cool thing about multimodality is that it can attend to multiple senses, which is sometimes necessary if a reader has a preference or need for one mode of communication over another. When creating multimodal texts, authors should *always* remember that not every reader will be exactly like them, whether in culture, society, class, race, gender, or ability. A text should be composed so that readers with limited vision, hearing, or touch—among other possible differences within an audience—can still interact with the text. For instance, imagine that you're filming someone who communicates through American Sign Language—would you film the person from the shoulders up, cutting their hands from the shot? No! As you analyze and compose multimodal texts, be careful to compose for as many different users with as many different backgrounds and abilities as possible.

Touchpoint: Examining a Simple Multimodal Text

We've looked so far at the individual modes and what they mean, but how do they work together in a text? We can analyze a sequence of elements (or groups of elements) and how they are juxtaposed (what we see before, with, or after) to help us create meaning. This Touchpoint asks you to consider the different modes at work in a sequence of video stills we created from a short video called "Stock Photo Love Story," originally designed in the early 2000s by Megan Sapnar Ankerson.

Ankerson used 1950s-era clip art to tell the story. In the original video, the opening screen included a black background with red all-caps text displaying the title, and a quirky game-show-style soundtrack accompanied the stock photos. The author intended this short video to be a fun exercise that also expressed frustration with the oppression of queer people. (In this version, we have replaced the original stock photos with similar ones because we couldn't track down permissions for the originals on this 15-year-old text. See Chapter 7 for more on permissions issues.)

Image 1:
Retro woman

Image 2:
Another woman

Image 3:
Yep, they're
in love

Image 4:
The last still in the
movie

Figure 1.17 Stills Representing *Stock Photo Love Story*
Images 1 through 4: RetroClipArt/Shutterstock

1. After viewing Image 1, did you expect to see another woman in the sequence in Image 2? Why is she here? Are these two women partners in the love story of the title?

2. In Image 3, how do these elements use gestural, spatial, visual, and linguistic modes of communication to create the meaning of love?

3. The last still in the movie in Image 4 shows a man. Why is he last in the sequence? What does his facial expression signify? What if he were smiling or frowning?

4. How does framing help tell this story effectively?

5. How would that story change if it had words (spoken or written—such as a different title) accompanying the stock photos and soundtrack?

Understanding Modes, Media, and Affordances

Let's say you want to share how much you adore your dog because your dog is so cute! You have hundreds of photos. These pictures are the *media* (singular *medium*) that you can share. The *medium* is the way your text reaches your audience. Other media you might use are video, speech, or paper (not a research paper per se, but the physical artifact on which a research paper would be printed).

Different media use different combinations of modes and are good at doing different things. We've all heard the expression "a picture is worth a thousand words." Sometimes it is much easier and more effective to use an image to show someone how to do something or how you are feeling. Say, for example, that the reason you wanted a picture of your dog is to show your friend in another state what the dog looks like (see **Fig. 1.18**). A picture will quickly convey more information in this situation than will a written description.

At other times, words may work better than images when we are trying to explain an idea because words can be more descriptive and to the point. It may take too many pictures to convey the same idea quickly (see **Fig. 1.19**).

Figure 1.18 Poor, Sad, Adorable Enid

Kristin Arola

Enid wakes me up at 4am on the day I'm leaving. Lies on my chest and stares at me. 22 hours later I get to my hotel. — in Saint Louis, MO.

Figure 1.19 Facebook Status Update Contextualizing Enid's Pitiful Look

Kristin Arola

In other situations where we are trying to communicate how something should be done, it can be more useful to create an animation or video that demonstrates the steps in a process than it is to write out instructions.

These different strengths and weaknesses of media (video, writing, pictures, etc.) and modes are called **affordances**. The visual mode *affords* us the opportunity to communicate emotion in an immediate way, while the linguistic mode *affords* us the time we need to communicate a set of detailed steps. Writer/designers think through the affordances of the modes and media available before choosing the right text for the right situation.

Keep in mind that modal affordances largely depend on how the mode is used and in what context. In other words, the strengths and weaknesses of each mode are dependent on, and influenced by, the ways in which the modes are combined, in what media, and to what ends. Their affordances can also be hindrances to some audiences you want to reach. For instance, the visually brief *emoji* can sum up an entire conversation in a single image or two, as in **Figure 1.20**, but those readers with less emoji literacy or fewer visual abilities might not understand what you mean.

Figure 1.20 Dumpster Fire, in Emoji

Dumpster fire was voted as the 2016 word (phrase, really) of the year by the American Dialect Society.

Dumpster: musicman/Shutterstock; fire: vectorEps/Shutterstock

CASE STUDY

Mapping Federal Spending

Although we've given you examples in this chapter of how each mode works on its own to communicate, we want to conclude with an extended example of how all the modes work together in a single multimodal text. Throughout this example, we're going to highlight some of the key concepts we want you to pay attention to.

The documents in **Figures 1.21 and 1.22** were created by the U.S. government to communicate information about nationwide economic recovery efforts. In the 1930s, the United States was suffering through a severe economic meltdown, known now as the Great Depression. To help alleviate the situation, President Franklin Delano Roosevelt (FDR) created the Works Progress Administration, which put millions of Americans to work repairing and updating the U.S. infrastructure, including building highways and fixing streets. The map in **Figure 1.21** shows a state-by-state and county-by-county textual and visual overview of street projects funded by the government.

- **Linguistic mode:** The words on this map describe what we are looking at.

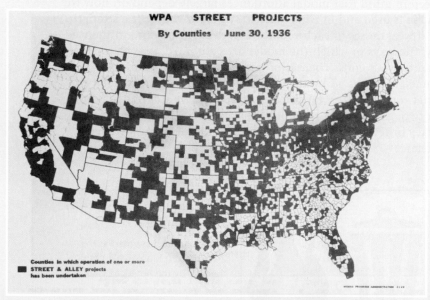

WPA STREET PROJECTS

By Counties   June 30, 1936

Counties in which operation of one or more
STREET & ALLEY projects
has been undertaken

Figure 1.21 Map of WPA Street Projects, 1936

The map, printed in the 1930s as part of the Works Progress Administration government recovery program, is a multimodal text.

- **Visual mode:** The shaded areas on the map visually represent locations where at least one project had taken place. Here, the color-coding shows us what areas received the most assistance.

- **Spatial mode:** The information is organized in map form, which positions the color-coded points according to US counties.

The visual and spatial modes work together to help us make comparisons between locations. For example, the densely shaded area in the Northeast, where the US population was most concentrated at the time, can be compared against the relatively barren spots in the West, where fewer people lived. A spatial representation of the states from 1936, when there were only forty-eight states, will be different from an 1803 map that focuses on the Louisiana Purchase, or from a 2011 map showing all fifty states. So in this map, the linguistic, visual, and spatial modes work together to show readers where street projects occurred in 1936.

What if the proportion of words and numbers (linguistic mode) to visual and spatial information had been changed to favor the linguistic elements? How could this map have been read differently? For instance, what if, instead of the street projects map, readers only saw large tables of data for each state, county, or project? (In fact, other parts of the WPA report from which the map is taken do include many data tables, such as the one shown in **Figure 1.22** on the next page.) The linguistic mode often *affords* readers specificity, exactness, and logical connections, but this can slow readers down as they work to make sense of the information. The visual mode, on the other hand, often can't be as detailed. We don't know from the map, for example, *how many* projects were completed in each area. But a visual presentation of complex information can allow readers to make quick comparisons. This ability for quick comparison is an **affordance** of the visual mode, particularly within the particular medium of the printed map.

We should also consider the affordances of the **media** available at the time of distribution. In 1936, radio and print (typically government reports or newspapers) would have been the primary media used to communicate to the public. Printing in color would have been prohibitively expensive, so black-and-white visuals and written text had to be used. In **Figure 1.23** (p. 27), we can see a more modern version of a similar report, a digitally based map from the former Recovery.gov website that illustrated economic recovery in the United States in 2009–2010. As FDR did in establishing the Works Progress Administration, President Barack Obama created the American Recovery and Reinvestment Act to stimulate job creation and repairs to the U.S. infrastructure during the Great Recession.

```
           VALUE OF MATERIALS, SUPPLIES AND EQUIPMENT
                PROCURED FOR WPA PROJECTS,
                   BY TYPES OF PROJECTS


                    Through May 30, 1936
```

Type of Project	Total Value Amount	Percent
TOTAL	$ 142,935,931	100.0
Highways, roads, and streets	45,952,629	32.1
Public buildings	27,297,802	19.1
Housing	67,172	0.1
Parks and playgrounds	20,601,596	14.4
Flood control and other conservation	6,817,343	4.8
Water supply and sewer systems	24,065,084	16.8
Electric utilities	586,279	0.4
Transportation	4,156,418	2.9
Educational, professional and clerical	2,944,215	2.1
Goods	3,822,563	2.7
Sanitation and health	3,287,372	2.3
Miscellaneous	3,337,458	2.3

Figure 1.22 Table of WPA Projects Data, 1936

A data table from a 1936 report showing the value of materials used in WPA projects.

Figure 1.23, which appears on the next page, is a contemporary version of the 1936 WPA report; it appears on a website and is interactive (as the highlighting and pop-up about New Mexico show). Its medium is a Web-based map as opposed to a print-based map. It uses linguistic, visual, and spatial modes of communication, just like the 1936 map does, but it also includes interactivity (a **gestural mode**). Below the map, there is an interactive search tool to find specific funding information by zip code. Because of the affordances of the Web (such as cheaper use of multiple colors and the use of electronic databases and interactivity), this map communicates a lot more information than a printed map in 1936 would have been able to communicate, and it reaches a much wider potential audience. These differences don't mean that the Web is a better medium than print—just that, due to the technological changes in the last century, the Web allows for more complex and detailed information to be conveyed to more people using a similarly sized map. It's expected that this information can be accessed online in the twenty-first century, and it would be foolish for the government to not use the affordances of the Web to reach its constituents.

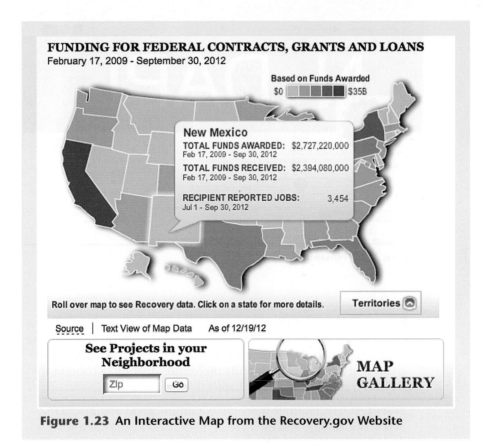

Figure 1.23 An Interactive Map from the Recovery.gov Website

Multimodal Affordances

The image of the map in **Figure 1.23** of the Case Study highlights at least four different modes of communication used in one text (linguistic, spatial, gestural, visual). Other texts, such as video interviews, combine all *five* modes, including the aural. One way to think about the different modes of communication is as a set of tools. You may not use all of them for a single project, because each mode has its own strengths and weaknesses in specific situations—just as a wrench is more useful in fixing a faucet than a hammer is. Like the tools in a toolbox, though, modes can sometimes be used in ways that weren't intended but that get the job done just as well (like a screwdriver used to pry open a paint can).

Together, the many modes that make up texts are useful in different situations. Multimodality gives writers additional tools for designing

Figure 1.24 NoDAPL Twitter Feed

effective texts. This is particularly true when writers are trying to create a single text that will appeal to the interests of a large, diverse group of readers. By understanding who their readers are, what they need to know, and how they will use the information, authors can create texts that satisfy a specific rhetorical situation, a concept we will cover in more detail in Chapter 2.

Every text uses multiple modes of communication and media to make its meaning, and each use of modes and media has affordances that help writer/designers make meaning through them. The Twitter profile in **Figure 1.24** has a lot of words (the linguistic mode), but the colors, layout, profile pictures, tweet sequence, and prominence of photo-rich tweets (visual and spatial modes) play a big role in how users read and understand each page. Also, the strict 140-character limit for tweets is an affordance of the site that *constrains* the way communication happens, offering lots of opportunity for quick broadcasts of ideas but little opportunity for discussion or civilized debate. But hashtags, which allow users to follow a single thread of ideas, are an affordance of multimodal websites that can help bring cohesion to the noise of social media.

⊙— **Touchpoint: Mode, Media, and Affordance in Everyday Texts**

To get a better sense of how prevalent multimodality is in all texts, and how different modes and media draw on their affordances to communicate to readers, collect and/or list texts of any kind that you come across in your daily schedule. These might include anything analog or digital, such as a receipt, flyer, business card, email, meme, website, book, video, song, advertisement, or photo. If you choose to make a list via social media, create a hashtag to keep track of them. If you're working as a class, use the hashtag to create a class record that you can analyze together.

Describe what modes and media the texts use. Count the number of modes that texts use, and see what patterns you can discover across the texts.

- Are they similar types of texts?

- Do they come from a similar time period, location, or publication?

- Are they making similar kinds of arguments?

- Which two texts are the most different from each other?

- How are the modes used in those texts? Which text uses the affordances of its media elements in the most surprising or unusual way? Are there any texts that are using modes and media in ways that seem counterproductive?

- How might you suggest the writer/designers of these texts revise?

write/design! assignment

Mapping Your Multimodal Process

This chapter has been about introducing you to the concepts of multimodality, which might be new for you, but it has also been about informing you that designing multimodal texts is based in a writing process that you are likely already familiar and comfortable with. Writers create with ease certain kinds of texts that they write often. Do you write a lot of emails? Facebook updates? Text messages to your friends or relatives? Do you write reports for work? Make presentations for clients? Write handwritten receipts for artwork you sell? Post forum notices to your fantasy football league? You likely do these tasks without thinking about them because they've become routine for you—you know the formula for writing the text, you know the people (or kinds of people) who will read this text, you know exactly how they will use it, and so on. So the process of writing has become automatic, something you don't stop to think about. This assignment is meant to help you realize the scope of things, interactions, and situations in which you write so that you can attend to the different processes, places, services, texts, and events that your writing functions within the next time you sit to write/design.

Think for a moment of the last major writing or design project you undertook: for a class, for an after-school group, for work, for a local organization or club, or just for fun—this project could be as simple as creating a flyer for your chess team, designing your wedding, writing a paper, or creating a website for your hobby.

Now that you have a project in mind, break it down into as many parts as possible and then visualize how those parts work to help (or hinder) you in completing that project. Create what's called a **gigamap**. Gigamaps are *BIG* maps used by designers to document everything they can about a system, which might include people, places, events, processes, services, tasks, texts, or experiences. In other words, gigamaps help you visualize your process.

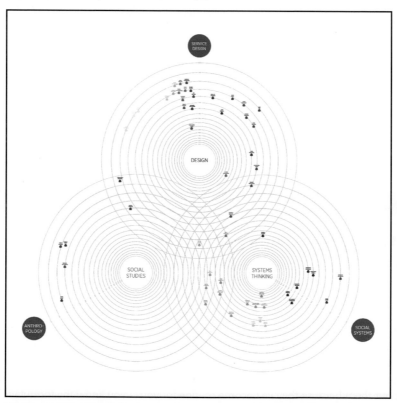

Figure 1.25 Manuela Aguirre's Gigamap of Research for Her Dissertation Project

Manuela Aguirre

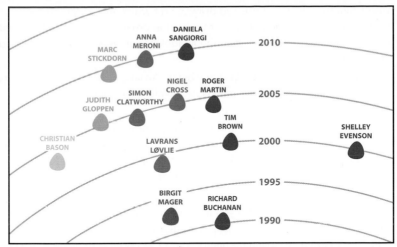

Figure 1.26 A Zoomed-in Portion of Manuela's Gigamap

The gigamap shows the years that different texts were published and their proximity in terms of disciplinary area (coded by color).

Manuela Aquirre

Gigamaps start out scrawled on really large pieces of paper—rolls of paper, if you have access to those, or you can use a dry-erase board, a giant piece of cardboard you might have handy, several poster boards taped together—as long as you don't start on a computer. (The process of mapping is more fruitful when you begin in analog form, and using paper is easier if you are collaborating with others, which often happens in design and large writing projects.) Do an image search online for gigamaps to see a variety of examples—they're too large to recreate in detail in this book, so we recommend exploring them in zoomed-in detail on a computer.

What do you include in your writing-process gigamap? Literally everything you can think of that relates to the *who-what-when-where-how* of the project you thought of a moment ago. We have adapted this assignment from Norwegian designer Birger Sevaldson, who created gigamapping, and we offer the following tips adapted from his guidelines to help you start:

- **Nothing is irrelevant:** Deactivate any filter of relevance to the task.
- **Nothing is uninteresting:** Even the smallest detail is interesting in its own right. Search and hunt for it. Look for the smallest details in a chain of events.
- **Strive for information richness:** Work toward a minimum of 100 entities on the map. If you don't have enough, stop filtering yourself or zoom out on your perspective.

- **Don't talk too much—write and draw:** Don't worry about wasting paper. Don't plan the mapping but allow it to develop organically. Don't get trapped in conversations on what the map should look like or what should be included; just include it.

- **Start anywhere.** Start to unfold at any detail. Avoid a central nucleus. Centers of gravity will be found or generated later. Avoid gravitating to hierarchical structures.

- **Activate existing knowledge:** Do not research information in the beginning. This will stop your flow before you even have started. Use your existing knowledge and map it out completely. Then identify what is insufficient and what is speculative and plan your information-gathering research accordingly.

- **Messy is good:** Do not let your inner designer take over the process too early. Let it be as messy as the reality you try to cope with.

- **Mix it up:** Strive to produce a deep map that contains many layers of different information. Allow for different ways of representing information in the map.

Finding and creating relations between different types of information that seem totally unrelated is one of the goals in gigamapping. Therefore, once you have a draft of your gigamap:

- **Create relations:** Use the mapping to create relations that are not there today. What relations should be created to make the system function better? A simple line is not sufficient. Arrows indicate directions of relations. Use additional font variations and color coding. Use other types of relations like proximity or sequencing. Put labels with small descriptive texts or other notes onto the relations and not only onto the entities.

- **Analyze and be critical:** Search for points and areas where there are possibilities for doing things better. Search for possible new relations, intervention points, and innovations in your writing system for this project.

- **Switch media:** Redraw the mapping on your computer and plot it out in large formats to continue working manually. Then repeat the process with new iterations.

- **Share with others:** Present your gigamap to others working on similar projects, in a studio, classroom, study space, work space, or so on, to explain what you've gleaned about your own writing and design process, and what you might improve on as you begin a new multimodal project. What surprised you about how your writing/designing process expanded? How were people, places, or tasks grouped? Why were those groupings important? And so on.

write/design! option: Multimodal Literacy Narratives

We bet you have plenty of experience with multimodality, whether you realize it or not. This assignment asks you to consider who you are as a multimodal reader, writer, and designer. Maybe there was a special book or teacher or performance you saw growing up that struck a chord with you? Or maybe it was an app you couldn't put down, or a game, or a TV series, or a movie? Tell a story about your use of and interaction with multimodality in the world.

Some questions that might help you think about a topic:

- Is there a particular text that stands out in your memory?
- Have you had a good (or bad) experience in learning to do something? Has it been in the classroom? Recreationally?
- What barriers to reading, writing, or technology have you encountered as a user?
- How does multimedia shape your ability to process and interpret information?
- What are the ways in which you use multimodal texts to navigate life in and outside of work or school?

Compose a narrative in whatever medium you want that includes any combination of modes—but it has to include at least three different modes at once. The story should tell about your engagement with multimodal texts. You can search for examples online using key phrases such as "literacy narrative" or "multimodal literacy narrative" or "technology narrative."

2 How Does Rhetoric Work in Multimodal Projects?

Have you ever been walking through town, and one flyer among the hundreds of flyers you see every day stands out so much that you can't help but stop and read it? Have you ever been rushing to a meeting when your favorite song starts playing, and you have to listen to it before you can enter the meeting? Have you ever found a website link or online video so exciting or funny that you have to immediately share it with your Facebook friends? These multimodal texts are captivating—they capture your attention and encourage you to interact with them and share them.

Chances are the multimodal texts that caught and held your attention are the ones that used the most effective design choices. These are the kinds of texts we want you to build. In this chapter you will learn how to analyze multimodal texts to discover how effective design choices are made for different texts in different situations.

Writer/designers have a wide variety of options for creating an effective text. What makes a text effective depends on a number of factors: What is the author's reason for creating the text? What audience is the author trying to reach? In what place, time, or situation is the text being created? Analyzing these factors will help you understand the projects of other writer/designers and will help you create your own multimodal texts.

Figure 2.1 An Effective Multimodal Flyer

This flyer on a school bulletin board caught Cheryl's attention. It was printed in color and in landscape orientation on 11" × 17" paper.

Courtesy of Steve Halle and Tara Reeser; created for the English Department's Publications Unit at Illinois State University

Rhetoric and Multimodality

When we talk about "effective" or "successful" texts, we're talking about rhetoric. Texts need to be created for a purpose, to persuade an audience toward change in some way; **rhetoric** is the study of making texts that effectively persuade an audience toward change. Echoing that old philosophical question—if a tree falls in the forest and no one is around to hear it, does it make a sound?—if a text doesn't induce change, then it isn't rhetorically successful. *Successful* multimodal persuasion is what this book is about.

You're probably familiar with some forms of persuading others to take action in favor of an author's viewpoint, such as when an advertisement tries to persuade us to choose a particular political candidate, a new summer outfit, a different brand of toothpaste, a recycling option, or a party to attend. Sometimes this change is more subtle and the action is less explicit, such as when reading a novel gives us a better understanding of the human condition (or simply causes us to relax), or—as in the Recovery.gov example in the Chapter 1 Case Study—when a government website teaches us more about how our taxes are spent and who they benefit.

As readers, we can choose whether to act based on how effectively a text persuades us. Let's think about a musical example. While a musician probably has many hopes for a song—that it speaks to people and is artistically meaningful, for example—one hope is that listeners will enjoy the song enough to purchase it. Whether listeners buy it depends on a lot of things: whether they like the song's lyrics, whether the song speaks to them in some way, whether they have the money, what format the song is available in, what technology they have for listening to the song, and the like. The song's author and producer had to think through all of these possibilities when creating and distributing the song. In the end, they have created a text that asks readers to make a choice. A particular listener's choice may be to do nothing (not to listen to or buy the song), but that's still a choice.

Our reactions typically depend on how well an author is able to address the **rhetorical situation**. The rhetorical situation is the set of circumstances in which an author creates a text. Authors have to pay attention to three factors if they want to be effective communicators: their intended **audience**, their **purpose** for communicating, and the **context** in which their text will be read. The author and genre are also important to consider, and we will address those concepts more in Chapter 3.

Analyzing a Rhetorical Situation

Understanding the situation in which an author composed a text can help us better understand a text's meaning and make judgments about its effectiveness. Who was the author? Why did he or she compose this text? When and where was it composed? Whom did the author want to reach? You may never know everything there is to know about the author's intended purpose or audience, and there isn't always (or ever) a "right" answer when analyzing a text. What we can do is learn how to analyze texts so that we can better guess, hypothesize, or even create a theory about how a text works and why.

Thinking through the rhetorical situation like this is called **rhetorical analysis**. Rhetorical analyses can result in texts of their

Figure 2.2 A Quick Rhetorical Analysis of a Parody

In a parody of the 2016 presidential debates, *Saturday Night Live* (a television show known for its comedic sketches) pokes fun at political candidates' supposed shortcomings (**purpose**)—Clinton's inability to relate to viewers and Trump's stalking of Clinton during the town hall debate—for viewers eager for comedy (**audience**) during a tough election cycle (**context**).

own (such as papers, presentations, or multimodal projects), but they can also function as research for your projects. If you can analyze how a text works, you can often apply that understanding to the design of your own text. A rhetorical analysis is a method of describing

- the *audience* an author wants to reach (the *who*);
- the *purpose* an author has for communicating to that audience (the *what* and *why*);
- the *context* in which an author wants to communicate that purpose or call for action (the *when* and *where*);
- the writing and design *choices* an author makes in a text that draw on audience, purpose, and context (the *how*).

These fundamental concepts (*audience*, *purpose*, and *context*) and questions (*who*, *what*, *when*, *where*, *why*, and *how*) help us perform a rhetorical analysis. Let's look at each of these areas in more depth now, followed by an in-depth look at how to analyze design choices to help determine rhetorical situation.

Audience

The audience is the intended readership for a text. There may be more than one intended audience, and there may also be more than one actual audience. Consider a pop-country song playing over the sound system at a mall. The songwriter's intended audience is likely pop-country fans, and her secondary audience may be pop or country music fans. Yet, in this context, the actual audience is anyone who happens to hear it.

There are many different types of audiences, such as *stakeholders*, *teachers*, *clients*, *readers*, and others, but all these terms refer to the person or people who are the intended readers or recipients of created texts. Often these terms are dependent on the rhetorical situation of a text. *Stakeholders* and *clients*, for instance, refer to people from the community or from an organization that a writer/designer is working for or with. They are the people asking (or paying) a writer/designer for a project, but they are not always the primary audience for it.

For example, Cheryl has worked on projects funded by the National Endowment for the Humanities (NEH), an agency of the U.S. government that supports humanities-based projects by providing federal grants to researchers. However, Cheryl made writing and design choices in consideration of her *primary audience*, the scholar-teacher communities in which she works because they were the ones who would most actively use the project. The project would also impact the public by making research more available to non-academics. So,

NEH is a *stakeholder* and *secondary audience* that expects certain kinds of reporting and deliverables on such projects in exchange for funding, and the public is a *secondary audience* of the project because they would benefit from its outcome.

In a rhetorical analysis, your job is to pay attention to the intended primary and secondary audiences. While it is not necessarily your job to consider how the text will function if read by those outside the intended audience, doing so can sometimes be illuminating.

When analyzing audience, consider these questions:

- Who is the intended audience?
- Who might be the secondary audience(s)?
- What values or opinions do the primary and secondary audiences hold?
- How does the author use design elements to appeal to these values or opinions?

◎— Touchpoint: **Analyzing Audience**

Figure 2.3 Hand-Drawn Flyer for Roller Derby

Nicole Schmidt

What audiences want from a text depends on their needs—in the case of the SNL skit example in **Figure 2.2** (p. 36), an audience wants comedic sketches about political figures. But what about other audiences' needs in different types of multimodal texts?

In **Figure 2.3**, a student in one of Kristin's classes drew this draft of a roller derby poster with pen and ink for a class assignment. The primary or intended audience would be parents of roller derby players, as signaled by the words, "Parent's Night: Be there or be square, 'rents!" But a secondary audience for this poster could be other students, teachers, business keepers,

Figure 2.4 Final Draft of a Roller Derby Flyer

Huizi Li

and sports enthusiasts in the small college town who like roller derby. Based on the hand-drawn design and the simple two-color graphics, what kinds of cultural and social values do you think the collective audiences of this poster might have? Would these audiences have anything in common with each other beyond roller derby?

What about **Figure 2.4**? It is also a roller derby flyer, but the writing and design are different than the hand-drawn example. Who are the primary and secondary audiences for this flyer? How might the different design values appeal to these different audiences? Or are the audiences between the two flyers actually that different? Even when a text is not designed with the language we may read or speak, we can often interpret its audience, purpose, and context based on the way multimodal elements are placed spatially. (These familiar usages are called genre conventions and will be discussed more in Chapter 3.)

Purpose

Purpose answers a single question: What is this text meant to accomplish? Describing a text's purpose may sound somewhat simplistic, yet it is important to consider a range of possible intentions—while there may be a large-scale purpose, there often are also secondary purposes. For example, a billboard for a local steakhouse has the primary purpose of attracting new clientele, but it may have the secondary purpose of solidifying existing customers' opinion of the restaurant as a fun-loving family establishment.

Purpose always plays a crucial role in analyzing and creating texts; without a clear purpose, a text is useless as a piece of communication. When analyzing purpose, consider these questions:

- What do you consider to be the overall intention for the text?
- What multimodal elements lead you to this conclusion?
- Might there be one or more secondary intentions? Why do you think so?

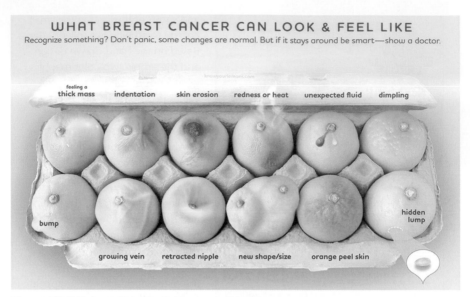

Figure 2.5 Breast Cancer Awareness Graphic

The Worldwide Breast Cancer organization used lemons as a visual replacement for breasts to achieve their educational purpose.

Image provided courtesy of Worldwide Breast Cancer, www.worldwidebreastcancer.org

The purpose of this breast cancer awareness graphic in **Figure 2.5** is fairly easy to determine: The lemons serve as visual representations for breasts, and each lemon is visually modified to show a symptom of breast cancer. The ad campaign, Know Your Lemons, was designed by Worldwide Breast Cancer, a nonprofit organization that uses multimodal design to educate and empower in ways beyond words, particularly for audiences that have low literacy rates or that face cultural and social taboos in talking about breasts or cancer.

◉— **Touchpoint: Analyzing Purpose**

Think Indian is a public service campaign that, according to the American Indian College Fund (AICF) website, "tells the story of how America's 32 accredited tribal colleges and American Indian students are combining traditional Native solutions with modern knowledge to solve contemporary problems." The ad in **Figure 2.6** was run in major media publications, such as the *New York Times Magazine* and *O*. The primary audience is donors, and the purpose of the ad is to solicit support for the AICF. A secondary audience could be people who identify as American Indians who may not have been aware that the AICF existed, or who want to attend college but weren't sure their ideas mattered. So, the primary stories, and purpose, presented in this campaign can have a secondary influence on this audience.

Consider the design of the ad and how it achieves the AICF's purpose. Perhaps conduct some research on the Think Indian campaign and the AICF and sketch out another possible version of this advertisement that has the same purpose as this one.

This bold white font contrasts sharply with the mute gray background, creating strong emphasis. Why would the idea of "native art made with looms and laptops" be such a strong focus of this ad? What does this say about tradition and technology and about how the purpose is being conveyed?

How does the pop of red against the black-and-white background and figure speak to the purpose of the text?

Notice the city skyline buildings are drawn in with a more traditional native pattern. How does this design, in contrast to the background image, identify a cultural context? What purpose does this design choice achieve?

This small blurb contains donation information. Does it support the primary or secondary purpose of the ad?

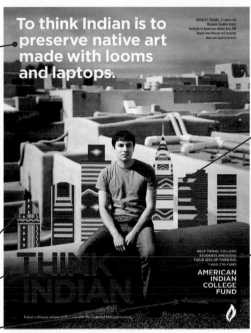

Figure 2.6 Annotated Ad for the Think Indian Campaign

The Think Indian campaign uses a mixture of multimodal elements to convey its purpose.

Courtesy of the American Indian College Fund

Context

Context can be quite broad. Context may be physical and consider the *where* the text is published or distributed (in an academic journal at a library, for example, or in the advertising section of a free weekly), *how* it is meant to be read (while sitting at a desk with one's full attention on the pages, or at a quick glance while flipping through a newspaper), *what* surrounds it (similar academic journal articles, other advertisements, an article about dining in Seattle), or *when* it was made (in a different decade or during a time of social change). In these ways, context is social and cultural, taking into account the values of a particular publication or culture or the important events taking place when the writer/designer was creating the text.

When analyzing context, consider these questions:

- What is the medium (print, app, Web, video, etc.)? Why do you think the author chose this particular medium over another one?

- Where did you find the text? What was the publication venue (book, newspaper, album, television, etc.)?

- What were the historical conventions for this type of text? What materials, media, or publishing venues were available at the time?

- What are the social and cultural connotations within the text? What colors, pictures, or phrases are used? What technologies does the text use?

- How will readers interact with this text? Will they read it on their phone or tablet while walking down the street? on a desktop computer in a public library? on a laptop in their backyard?

It often feels like context is the widest of possible lenses to analyze a text with. The Web comic by Robot Hugs, "No, We Won't Calm Down—Tone Policing Is Just Another Way to Protect Privilege," lets us examine the challenges of context in rhetorical situations. The comic defines tone policing, a tactic used to derail conversations

Figure 2.7 Robot Hugs, "No, We Won't Calm Down"

Robot Hugs's Web comic on tone policing can be viewed in its entirety at http://www.robot-hugs.com/tone-policing/.

by attacking someone's tone or emotions because you'd rather not engage in their argument. (In the description that follows, we use gender-neutral pronouns. We discuss why in the next Touchpoint assignment.)

Figure 2.7 shows one character from the comic expressing appreciation that ze has a circle of colleagues (say, in hir cluster of colleagues during a collaborative work session) with whom ze can discuss issues about work life that make hir sad, angry, vehement, and so on, whereas in other situations that contain different people (say, in a meeting with hir colleagues and supervisors to present a report to external stakeholders) hir anger, glee, or other affects may need to be redirected toward pitching the presentation for the audience. Rhetorically, two different contexts require two different tones, and being able to analyze the myriad ways that context plays a role in our communications is important to ensuring that those communications are effective.

◉— Touchpoint: **Analyzing Context**

You may have noticed that we used gender-neutral pronouns: *ze* instead of *she* or *he* and *hir* instead of *him* or *her*. Many readers, ourselves included, may have looked at the character in **Figure 2.7** and assumed it was female. The socio-cultural contexts in which we authors have grown up (female, all in our early forties now, North American, primarily White, with one of us being part American Indian) incline us to assume that any character with the visual feature of long hair—in this case, long enough to pull into a bun—is feminine and therefore female. But we certainly know that plenty of men wear their hair long, too. So, because we don't really know the context of this character, and the comic doesn't explicitly suggest a gender (nor does it need to), we've decided to apply a more capacious, gender-neutral pronoun to them. ("Them" and "they," as used with Robot Hugs, have also become favored third-person, gender-neutral pronoun choices in recent years.)

The Web browser extension Jailbreak the Patriarchy, designed by Danielle E. Sucher, genderswaps all pronouns and gendered words on a website. This tiny Web app replaced "him" with "her," "mother" with "father," and so on. In the cultural and social contexts in the United States, this small linguistic change can have a big impact. Just knowing that such an extension exists—or that Suchor was the first female graduate of a computer programming collective in New York City that places many of its alumnae in top start-up or industry jobs—might inspire a young adult to learn to program and to change the world.

Do an online search for Jailbreak the Partriarchy and try it out on a Chrome browser, or if you don't have access to that technology, take any text that includes people, such as a superhero comic or book cover, and quickly redesign it (using whatever materials you have handy—a rough sketch is fine) to swap the genders in the design and the writing. Note that genders don't have to be binary—male or female—they can also be fluid or androgynous, like the character in **Figure 2.7**. How does this genderswap change the context of the piece? Does it change the message of the communication at all? Does it extend the meaning to new audiences, or does it restrict the message in unexpected ways?

Analyzing Design Choices

One of the ways we can better understand how writer/designers communicate meaning through multimodal texts is to examine its design elements. As we look more closely at the types of choices a designer makes, we focus on six key design concepts: **emphasis**, **contrast**, **color**, **organization**, **alignment**, and **proximity**. These terms aren't the only ones you could use to talk about choices—you may come up with some terms on your own or in collaboration with your colleagues—but they give you a start. We ask you to think about how such choices are or are not effective in each particular rhetorical situation. Below we define these terms and provide a few analytical examples. We put them all together, alongside audience, purpose, and context, in a Case Study at the end of this chapter.

Emphasis

In speech or writing, emphasis means stressing a word or a group of words to give it more importance. In visual texts, it means the same thing; emphasis gives certain elements greater importance, significance, or stress than other elements in the text, which can guide your reading of the text as a whole.

When analyzing an image for emphasis, we pay attention to what we notice first and then ask ourselves why. Look back to the Think Indian ad we showed in the Touchpoint activity on pages 40–41. Where is your attention visually drawn? What strategies does the writer/designer use to emphasize this element? Notice what happens in **Figure 2.8**: when the advertisement is changed to black and white, the words *THINK INDIAN* are no longer emphasized. Instead, the focus shifts to the white text at the top left, emphasized because of its contrast against the gray background. The emphasis also shifts from the words and the drawn building images to the student. Given the endless possibilities, why do you think this text's designer chose to make *THINK INDIAN* a large, red, all-caps typeface?

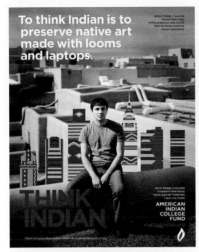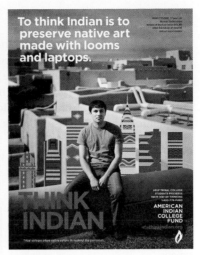

Figure 2.8 Design Choices in Think Indian Ads

Changing the color, size, and shape of the typeface and images impacts how we perceive which elements are emphasized in the whole text.

Courtesy of the American Indian College Fund

Contrast

Contrast is the difference between elements, where the combination of those elements makes one element stand out from another. Contrast can be determined by comparing elements in a text. Color, size, placement, shape, and content can all be used to create contrast in a text. Contrast plays a large role in emphasis, in that the most contrasted element often appears to be the most emphasized. See **Figure 2.9**, which contrasts the size of two elements, focusing our attention on the largest one that takes up the most space. Consider, too, **Figure 2.10**. Think about what connotations the word "dream" creates for you. Now, compare your conception of "dream" with the image here. How does this image contrast with your connotation of the word?

Figure 2.9 Contrast in Size

Figure 2.10 A Dream or a Nightmare? A Lesson in Contrast

Color

Color can be extremely helpful when determining emphasis in a visual text. Visual emphasis can be accorded to how bold or large, or how much black compared to the white or gray background, is used. Although color theory indicates that different cultures interpret colors differently around the world, warm colors are usually read as more emotionally intense—think fire, sun, and summer—and are used to elicit emotional reactions in audiences. Cool colors are usually read as calming and are used to create less emphasis than warm colors in a visual composition.

Warm colors such as reds and oranges command more attention than cooler colors like blues and greens.

We tend to associate cool colors like blues and greens with water, leaves, cool temperatures, and the sky.

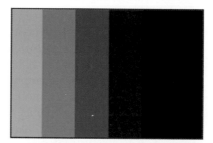

Color doesn't have to mean red, orange, or blue—black and white are colors, too.

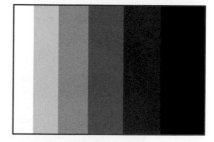

Figure 2.11 Color Options

Analyzing a text for color means noticing not only what colors are being used, but to what effect. Do the colors create a certain mood or feeling? Do they work to emphasize a particular element? Or do they work to highlight certain elements on the page in relation to each other?

Organization

Organization is the way in which elements are arranged to form a coherent unit or functioning whole. You can talk about an organization of people, which puts people into a hierarchy depending on their job title and department, or about organizing your clothes, which might involve sorting by color and type of garment. You can also talk about organizing an essay, which involves arranging your ideas so as to make the strongest argument possible. Or you can talk about organizing the multimodal elements of a website to support the purpose of the text.

Consider the most recent redesign of your favorite social media site. Where did the designers move the direct-messaging feature? The group chats? The media upload buttons? The editing features? How long did it take you to reorient your gestural navigation to find the information you wanted? Helping users understand the organizational structure of a text is important to ensure audience engagement.

Figure 2.12 is from an experimental webtext in which the author proposes creating a memorial for animals harmed during the 2010 BP oil spill when the *Deepwater Horizon* oil rig exploded in the Gulf

Figure 2.12 Organization in an Experimental Webtext

Video content is linked to touchpoints organized along a key driving route and represented on a map.

Sean Morey/Kairos from Morey, Sean. (2017). Deepwater horizon memorial: Roadkill tollbooth. *Kairos: A Journal of Rhetoric, Technology, and Pedagogy* 21(2). Retrieved March 16, 2017, from http://kairos.technorhetoric.net/21.2/topoi/morey/index.

of Mexico. This memorial would be created along the Florida toll-road and attached to tollbooths along the way. The author uses a map with touchpoint icons overlayed on locations of tollbooths, and users can click to find videos that support his argument. For readers unfamiliar with this route, the author begins with the word *Start* on the location of the oil spill, and *End* in Key West at the hypothetical ending to the memorial. Organization is important to consider when you design so that you do not sacrifice usability for aesthetics. In this example, the author manages to satisfy both usability and aesthetic practices by providing a clearly marked organizational structure.

Alignment

Alignment literally means how things line up. A composition that uses alignment to best effect controls how our eyes move across a text. Even if we're working with a text that is all words, every piece of it should be deliberately placed. A centered alignment—an easy and popular choice—causes our eyes to move around the space with less determination, as we move from the end of one line and search for the beginning of the next one. A justified alignment stretches the content so that it is evenly distributed across a row; thus the left and right margins remain consistent. This is a popular choice for newspapers because it can make a large amount of text appear neat and orderly. A strong left alignment gives us something to follow visually—even elements that contrast in size can demonstrate coherence through a single alignment. A strong right alignment creates a hard edge that connects disparate elements. Grouping things in a clear and interesting way can be useful.

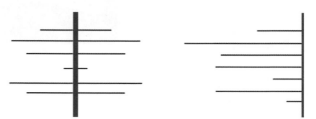

Figure 2.13 Differences in Alignment

Proximity

Proximity means closeness in space. In a visual text, it refers to how close elements (or groupings of elements) are placed in proximity to each other and what relationships are built as a result of that spacing. The relationships created by the spacing between elements help readers understand the text, in part because readers might already be familiar with similar designs of other texts. Proximity can apply to any kind of element in a visual text, including words and images, or to elements of an audio text, such as repeating rhythms or the verses and chorus.

Analyzing proximity in a text means thinking about how elements are grouped together, where they are placed on the page or screen in relation to one another, and how placement suggests purpose. One way to figure out how elements are grouped together into like categories or relationships is to squint your eyes and count how many major groups you see.

How many groupings do you see on the book cover in **Figure 2.14**? Book covers are designed to sell books to readers; they have to present information and content in an interesting, visual, and coherent way. The biggest text—in large, bold letters on two lines—is at the top of the cover. This is the book title and the most important information. Placed underneath the book's title are the names of the book's editors. You can tell that the titles and names are related because they appear close to each other. The tan line in which the editors' names are presented also clusters these names together. At the same time, the information that appears below the tan line—the publisher and table of contents (TOC)—uses the same color scheme as the editors' names, which is an additional

Figure 2.14 The Cover of an Interactive e-Book

Courtesy of Ryan Trauman

technique used to create relationships. The title and editors are grouped by physical proximity on the page, and the editors, publisher, and table of contents are grouped by proximity of color.

Proximity is also relevant when managing multimedia elements in an animated text such as an audio or video file. Consider how a soundtrack element and a filmic element might need to be presented simultaneously to achieve a text's purpose. Or, think about how annoying it is to the viewer when the audio and video don't sync properly. The proximity of the multimedia elements matters a lot to the audience's understanding of purpose.

◉— Touchpoint: **Analyzing a Website's Rhetorical Design Choices**

Try the exercise here to analyze a website (and if you want to see how *we* analyze a specific home page, read the Case Study in this chapter, then come back to this Touchpoint activity). Visit your favorite website or app—one whose purpose you are familiar with—and notice the information on the landing page. Why do you think it was chosen? What does it say about the primary intended audience and its needs? Take note of the design choices that stand out to you, paying attention to the following:

- What elements does the design of the website *emphasize*? The logo? A certain picture? The navigation bar? Why would the design of these elements speak to the intended audience?

- How is *contrast* used on the page? Does the use of contrast help to emphasize certain elements? Does it create a certain feeling or help the designer reach a certain audience?

- How do certain *colors* emphasize certain elements or encourage certain emotional and cultural responses?

- Notice the *organization* of elements on the page. What comes first? What comes last? Why do you think the designer chose this order? How does it assist in communicating the context and purpose of the site?

- What elements are *aligned* on the page? Does this alignment help you navigate the page? How does this choice help the designer communicate the site's purpose?

- How are elements positioned in *proximity* to one another? Why did the designer place certain elements in close relation and others farther apart? What does this proximity communicate about the website's primary purpose?

Writing and Designing Rhetorically

We began this chapter by discussing the rhetorical situation and then moved on to the design choices. However, we can also work the other way around—starting with an analysis of the design choices so as to understand the rhetorical situation. Don't be surprised if analyzing a text's design causes you to go back and say more about the audience, purpose, and context of the text—form and content work together in multimedia texts. Keep in mind that using rhetorical analysis to understand a text may result in a favorable opinion of the text but may also illuminate various problems—the rhetorical analysis may help explain why the text has that "wow" factor, or why it doesn't.

CASE STUDY

Analyzing the WSU Website

Our goal in this rhetorical analysis of the Washington State University website is to figure out what types of **design choices** were used to effectively respond to a particular rhetorical situation and convey the text's **purpose** to the **audience** in a specific **context**.

Figure 2.15 (p. 52) shows the home page of the Washington State University (WSU) website. This text, like most university home pages, has two main **purposes**: (1) to brand the university in a positive light by showcasing its newsworthy items, and (2) to serve as the portal to a large amount of additional information about the university. These dual purposes are what we would expect from a text of a university website home page these days. University home pages tend to include attractive images and links to information about the university's research endeavors, its academic and athletic programs, its admissions and financial aid policies, its students and faculty, and its location.

The **audience** for the home page is the intended readership: people interested in WSU, including current or potential students and their parents, alumni, faculty and staff, funding or government agencies, and donors. A good designer would try to think of all the different reasons to visit the WSU home page and then design the page for these various users.

Figure 2.15 The Front Page of the Washington State University Website (2017), Featured on a Laptop Courtesy of Washington State University

The WSU home page is organized into two rows of information. The first row is a white bar that includes the WSU logo, a menu, and a search function. The second row includes a photo, a link to a news item that explains the photo, and a menu of recent news items by date. This simple **organization** is referred to as *flat design* because it minimizes the number of elements that appear on a starting screen. In this particular design, the elements are grouped in close **proximity** to indicate the different sub-purposes each grouping has, and to make it seem like there are fewer blocks of information to choose from. Designers have begun using flat design to prevent audiences from feeling confused or overwhelmed on their sites. From an aesthetic standpoint, users and designers seem to like this trend, but organizationally, it can make finding information difficult.

Analyzing a text within its *historical* and *technological* **context** is important—as our goals, technologies, and media affordances change over time, so does the effectiveness of a particular design. Compare the 1997 WSU site **(Fig. 2.16)** with the redesigned site from 2000 **(Fig. 2.17)** and 2010 **(Fig. 2.18)**. The assumed size of the screens that **audiences** would use to view websites has changed radically in the last twenty years, as we have moved from midsized, low-resolution monitors to large, high-resolution desktop and laptop screens, and now the use of handheld devices with high resolutions and tiny screens has radically increased. The version of the WSU website in **Figure 2.15** was created in 2017 and is intended for

Figure 2.16 1997 Version of the WSU Website

Courtesy of Washington State University

Figure 2.17 2000 Version of the WSU Website

Courtesy of Washington State University

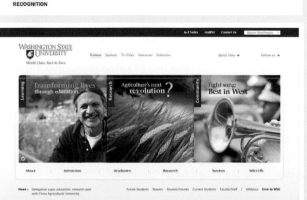

Figure 2.18 2010 Version of the WSU Website

Courtesy of Washington State University

Figure 2.19 2017 WSU Website, Featured on a Mobile Phone

Courtesy of Washington State University

viewing on a computer or mobile phone (see **Fig. 2.19**). This is called *responsive design* because it *responds* to the device it's being read on. Understanding the technological and historical contexts of multimodal texts helps us analyze how and why a text is designed for particular audiences and contexts.

The **purpose** of public university websites like WSU has also changed over time—the earlier sites were intended to be portals to attending and working at WSU, while the most recent site design shifts importance to daily news stories that exemplify the university's intellectual contributions to society. When the site was redesigned to be responsive, Web design conventions had shifted to focus on visuals as the primary mode of communication.

The photo shown in **Figure 2.15** is given primary visual **emphasis** on the WSU home page from 2017. Simply put, it takes over the entire screen. These visual changes can also be noted in the use of **color** throughout the website's history. In early examples, crimson was employed to the point of overuse (in retrospect) to draw our attention. The color makes cultural references to the university's official colors and is associated with grabbing attention (think stop signs). In more recent examples, crimson is still used, but more judiciously, to draw our attention to important information, such as the news-item box that is set over the photo on the left.

By emphasizing something bright, colorful, and positive (two women at work in a bright lab setting), the website conveys the feeling of a productive research environment relevant to a research-intensive university. The primary linguistic element—the words "Taking a shot at preventable deaths"—is **aligned** center on both screen sizes, drawing our attention to the importance of these words.

Thus, the page is not too busy, like earlier writing-heavy versions were, and the **audience** can easily see the site's **purpose**, to promote the university's intellectual contributions to society. In **contrast**, important information about the university, such as a directory of emails, is hidden in the "hamburger" (the tiny three-lined menu in the upper-left corner) on a mobile user's phone.

With the website's focus on a single photo and less on written text, **alignment** is a less prominent design choice. But if we scroll down (see **Fig. 2.20**), we find more linguistic modes represented, which have strong left alignments that create a multi-columned effect. The boxes on this part of the site—such as Visit, Inquire, and Apply in the left column—are also aligned horizontally along a central axis.

In **Figure 2.20**, the **organization**, **alignment**, and **color** of visual and linguistic elements designed into two columns as well as the **proximity** of certain elements suggests how the information is grouped. For instance, the "Find my field of study" search box is anchored by white space above

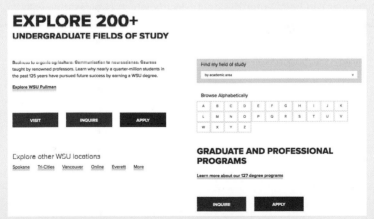

Figure 2.20 Featured Information on the 2017 WSU Website

Strong use of alignment and color create focal areas for audiences on an information-rich website.

Courtesy of Washington State University

it, which draws the attention of the **audience**. Its position, aligned horizontally with the undergraduate program descriptions and left-aligned with the "Graduate and Professional Programs" header, signal that this search box will help users find *either* undergraduate or graduate fields of study because it inhabits the same proximal distance from both major categories on this screen. Notice, too, how there is white space (a form of color) surrounding "Explore other WSU locations" and its menu of location options immediately underneath. These two lines of information are meant to stand together while also standing apart from the rest of the information on this screen, using white space as a proximal buffer to other groupings. These design choices highlight the key **purposes** for the relevant **audiences** of this particular part of the site: undergraduate and graduate students interested in enrolling in the university.

Of course, the design of this site, while engaging, isn't always as useful as it could be. As we explored this website ourselves, we couldn't find the email directory listing all employee and student email addresses, which is one of the main reasons some **audiences** use a university website. Key information for university website audiences is often buried. Such placement of information (related to the **organization** or page layout) indicates that "buried" items are less important. This can be a serious drawback of flat designs that tend to hide information in subsequent pages or in pages that endlessly scroll. Performing an analysis of a text's rhetorical situation and design choices can help writer/designers decide which choices they will make in their own texts.

write/design! assignment

Designing a Rhetorical Analysis

We talked a lot in Chapter 1 about the variety of texts that are multimodal, and we've talked a lot in this chapter about how those texts make meaning to specific audiences through design choices an author has made. Now it's your turn to practice analyzing a multimodal text. This book moves you toward becoming an author of multimodal texts, so for this assignment, we encourage you to work with the kinds of texts that you will want to make in the near future—perhaps ones you are expected to produce for a class, event, or client, or just something you want to make for yourself.

1. **Find an example** of a multimodal text similar to the type you want to design. Your choice of text/artifact for this project is nearly unlimited, unless you have been assigned a specific kind of text from your clients or teacher. If you get to choose any kind of text to analyze, the best projects usually come about through selecting a topic that is of personal interest to you *and* that is rich in the sort of rhetorical moves and design choices it uses.

2. **Analyze it** using the key concepts you learned in this chapter, with the following questions to guide you (but feel free to expand on these suggestions). Alternatively, you can revisit a text you have created in the past and perform a rhetorical analysis on the project to discover, in retrospect, whether it was as rhetorically successful as you had intended.

    Audience: Who is the intended audience? Who might be the secondary audience(s)? What values or opinions do the primary and secondary audiences hold? Does the author appeal to these values or opinions in any way?

    Purpose: What do you consider to be the overall intention for the text? What leads you to this conclusion? Are there secondary intentions? Why do you think so?

    Context: What is the medium (print, app, Web, video, etc.)? Why do you think the author chose this particular medium over another one? What was the publication venue (book, newspaper, album, television, etc.)? What were the historical, social, and cultural contexts and values of the audience and publication? What technologies does the text use?

    Design choices: What elements do you see first? Last? Why do you think the designer chose this order? What elements are emphasized through color or some other way? How is contrast used? What elements are aligned? How and why are elements positioned in relation to one another?

3. **Make notes** on your answers to these questions. As you go through these questions, you will want to have your sample text in front of you. Feel free to make your notes multimodally: record yourself talking, draw pictures, type textual notes on top of an image on your computer screen, even create a gigamap like you did in the Chapter 1 Write/Design! assignment and use large sheets of paper to document your analysis.

4. **Reflect on the text's situation**: After you have completed your initial analysis of your sample texts, read through your notes and decide which parts of your analysis are best supported by the rhetorical and designerly evidence you've collected. Ask yourself what the purpose of your text is and how all the rhetorical and design choices help achieve that purpose. What key examples or elements in the text help you explain its rhetorical situation? How would you organize these elements to explain the text's rhetoric to someone else?

5. **Consider the presentation format:** Now, think about your *own* rhetorical situation as a designer of a multimodal analysis. How you might present your analysis to someone else—would they prefer it all written down in an essay? Or as a spreadsheet with the key concepts as column headers? Or as a poster? How can you pull out the main evidence from your analysis to create a cohesive text that presents your reading to an audience? Rather than relying solely on words, this approach allows you to use the affordances of each mode to deliver your argument most effectively.

   For example, if you are interested in how acquaintances construct their identity through images on Instagram or text on Snapchat, creating an annotated slideshow of posts would work most efficiently for presenting details of your text.

6. **Compose your multimodal argument** on the effectiveness of these choices using whatever tools or modes are most effective for your own rhetorical situation and then present your multimodal analysis to that audience.

write/design! option: Writing a Rhetorical Analysis

This option asks you to complete a detailed and persuasive analysis of a text and present it as a written essay using quotations from the original text. Quotations might include both written text and other multimodal elements such as images. Nearly any multimodal text will work as the basis of your analysis, but here are a few ideas: a single photo or series of photos (such as the photo essays available in online news sites like CNN or the *New York Times*), an advertising campaign, a website, a movie or TV episode, a series of Instagram filters, a collection of tattoos, a radio program's use of sound effects, the signage and branding on your campus, or something else entirely.

Follow the same questions as those posed in **Step 2** of the first option (p. 57) listed previously so that you analyze the rhetorical situation of your text based on its written and designed content. When writing up your analysis, plan to use several specific examples from the text in your critique. Consider including images, screenshots, quotes, or other ways of showing your readers pieces of the original text to support your argument. If you are analyzing sound, a gesture, or something that cannot easily be represented in a written essay, take care to describe it in specific detail so your reader can understand your analysis. Remember that you are trying to reveal something about the rhetorical and design choices within the text that perhaps your audience didn't notice or hadn't thought about. Help your reader see what you see in that text.

3 Why Is Genre Important in Multimodal Projects?

One of the biggest lessons we've learned as authors and teachers is the value of learning by writing for real audiences with real-world purposes—what the New London Group would call *situated practice*. That is, if you compose in the different media, modalities, and genres you encounter in a specific rhetorical situation, with its particular social and cultural expectations, you can communicate more persuasively. At the heart of excellent writing/designing lies an author's explicit use (or breaking) of genre conventions within a rhetorical situation. In this chapter, we focus on understanding the messy concept of **genres** and how authors choose their genres and work within **genre conventions**. We will perform a **genre analysis** on a sample set of texts (which builds on rhetorical analysis from Chapter 2), and you can use that information to decide which kind of text *you* want to compose as an author within your own rhetorical situation.

Genre and Multimodality

One of the best ways to begin thinking about a multimodal project is to see *what* has already been said about a topic you are interested in (or have been assigned) as well as *how* other authors have designed their texts on that topic. For instance, you may want to create a text about how students use technology to enhance their learning experience. Before getting started, you'll need to know what's already been said about that topic—an exploratory process that's similar to what you'd do when writing a research paper. Researching your topic is the *what* part of the equation (in other words, figuring out *what* you want to say).

While you're researching your topic, you'll also need to explore *how* other authors are presenting that topic. What combinations of communicative modes do you see in other authors' texts about your topic? What design choices are they making? What genres are they using? Unless your teacher or client has assigned you

Figure 3.1 A Recipe

This genre of food writing features step-by-step instructions and can be found in different forms on food blogs, websites, print cookbooks, or newspapers. Recipes can also be passed down verbally through communities.

Angela Buchanan

a specific genre to work within, you'll want to research multiple genres in multiple media outlets—both academic (texts you'd find in a library database listed under "peer reviewed") and popular (texts you'd find on websites such as YouTube or in book-stores, trade magazines like *Good Housekeeping* or *Wired*, personal blogs, brochures in doctors' office waiting rooms, ads on the sides of buses, etc.). You'll see a different combination of modes and different design choices in each of these texts, depending on the rhetorical goals of the publisher and the author's rhetorical situation.

When examining the *how* of your topic, you'll need to ask yourself:

- How do other authors present your topic?
- Which of their texts seems to address its rhetorical situation most effectively?

Author

Like the terms we used in Chapter 2 to refer to *stakeholders, teachers, clients,* or *audiences*—meaning the people who are the readers or recipients of the texts we create—the terms *writer, designer,* **author**, and *composer* mean the people who make the texts. In this chapter, we shift from focusing on readers who perform rhetorical analyses of a completed text to authors (or designers or composers or writers) who perform rhetorical analyses in order to understand the circumstances under which their text needs to be created.

These terms, like those for audiences, are often dependent on the rhetorical situation for a text. But they are *also* dependent on the genre of your multimodal project. Don't worry, we aren't going to quiz you on which author term goes with which genre. We use them interchangably sometimes. But know that some folks will have a preference for which term you use with them. Just ask, if you're in doubt. And if you have a preference, indicate it to clients or other stakeholders as well as on your project, résumé, or business card.

Sometimes authorship will be quite clear—say, in the case of a signed letter to the editor—while at other times you will have to make an informed guess and rely on the implied author. Consider, for example, a visual advertisement for Starbucks. A team of designers (the actual author) composed it, yet the audience assumes Starbucks (the implied author) is the one sending the message. There are other texts, such as a concert flyer, for which you likely will have no idea who the actual author is, but you can probably say a lot about the implied author based on the design of the text.

In the case when you are authoring a text, you know exactly who the author is, of course. But you also have a rhetorical situation in which you have to choose your design elements and genre carefully, so as to best reach the audience you intend. When you're composing, you can ask yourself these questions to make sure you are achieving your purpose and establishing credibility as an author.

- How do you (as an author) establish personal or brand credibility? What multimodal elements make your text trustworthy? Does it matter for your audience?

- Does the author (you or the brand) have a certain reputation? Does the text work to support this reputation, or does it work to alter this reputation? Which is needed in this particular rhetorical situation?

- What other types of information in the text (historical, biographical, genre-based, research-based) will help you convince readers of your or the brand's credibility, character, and reputation?

Figure 3.2
Wikipedia Home Page

Wikipedia is renowned for its collaboratively authored and edited encyclopedia entries.

As with the Starbucks example, sometimes the fact that you are the author is irrelevant to the composition process if the audience doesn't care or doesn't need to know that you are the actual author—because the audience sees a corporation, group, or some other collaborative entity as the implied author. So as author in that situation you need to analyze the mission and vision (the purpose) of the group you are speaking, designing, or writing for and work seamlessly as part of the whole. Your rhetorical analysis skills will come in handy just as much when you are writing/designing as they do when you are reading mul timodal texts.

Genre

Authors are often responsible for suggesting or choosing genre. You've probably heard the term *genre* used to talk about static categories of texts in broad terms. Sometimes genre relates to a text's medium, such as newspapers, albums, or movies, and sometimes we use it to refer to more specific items within a genre, such as horror, romantic comedy, Western, and so on. Generally speaking, audiences expect something from newspapers that they do not expect from movies, and they expect something from horror movies that they do not expect from romantic comedies. This traditional understanding of genre helps us recognize how to group similar texts and understand their communicative purpose.

Understanding Genre Conventions

Genres aren't just static categories; they can morph according to the rhetorical situation, which may include local culture, social agreements and expectations, historical time period, author of the text, audience for the text, and many other influences. Genres are dynamic, but most genres have formal features that tend to remain the same in each use. These features are the **genre conventions**—the features that audiences expect from a text. Conventions of a horror movie, for example, include dark lighting and ominous music.

Antarctica (Small Map), 2016

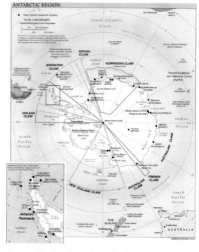

Antarctic Region (Political), 2001

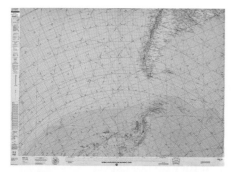

Antarctica Global Navigation and Planning Chart (Sheet G-24), 1970

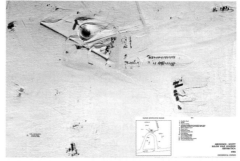

Antarctica South Pole Aerial View, from Amundsen-Scott South Pole Station, 1983

Figure 3.3 CIA Maps of Antarctica

The University of Texas Libraries, The University of Texas at Austin

Readers expect a map, as one type of genre, to be a spatial and visual arrangement of a place with labels for major points of interest. The whole point of maps is for readers to be able to orient themselves geographically (in most cases) to a destination. Maps conventionally include notations for scale, distance, and direction, and also include a legend that defines icons used in the map. Other genre conventions for maps are a title (which indicates its purpose), the name of the cartographer, the date of production, and the projection used in the map. Check out the four maps included in **Figure 3.3**, all produced by the U.S. Central Intelligence Agency at different times and for different purposes, but all focused on the continent of Antarctica. Each of them includes the essential genre conventions for maps mentioned in this paragraph.

As the varying designs of the maps in **Figure 3.3** indicate, genres often contain **subgenres**, or groups of similar genres that all fall under the same category. We know that all of the figures shown are maps, even though the genre conventions are designed in different ways for each map. Some map subgenres include artistic, relief, geologic, Z-dimension, street, general reference atlas, cartograms, abstract, thematic, schematic, and topographic. (We promise there won't be a quiz! We're just indicating the breadth of map subgenres, so we won't define each here.) Each subgenre of map is designed to fulfill a different rhetorical situation, but all include the essential genre conventions of maps, unless a cartographer's goal is specifically to break the conventions for some artistic or rhetorical purpose.

For instance, one reason a cartographer might want to break convention is to show something that would otherwise be missing or distorted in a map design. Maps typically indicate their *projection*, which refers to their representation of area, distance, direction, and shape. Projection is created based on longitude and latitude and deciding how to represent a spherical planet on a flat, rectangular piece of paper. One of the best-known is the Mercator projection, which unnaturally distorts the size of certain areas, making them appear much larger or smaller than they actually are (see **Fig. 3.4** on p. 66). Many cartographers and critics have suggested different projections that accommodate a more accurate representation of area on maps, such as the Gall-Peters projection, which shows the African continent much larger than in the Mercator map (see **Fig. 3.5**). Some argue that this rendering corrects a false, Eurocentric power dynamic. Or sometimes, because of the situation, your focal point on the map isn't the equatorial perspective—with the northern hemisphere at the top and southern hemisphere at the bottom of the flat map, respectively—which we typically see in many world maps.

Figure 3.4 **A Mercator Map**

Among other distortions, this map distorts Antarctica to be larger than the rest of the continents put together.

VanHart/Shutterstock

Figure 3.5 **A Gall-Peters Projection Map**

This map projection looks purposefully distorted but actually has no distortion at 45° latitude north and south.

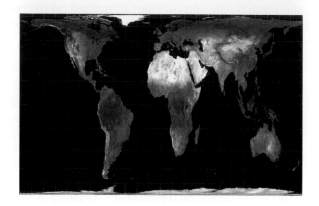

Figure 3.6
An Orthographic Projection Map

Matt Cooper/Shutterstock

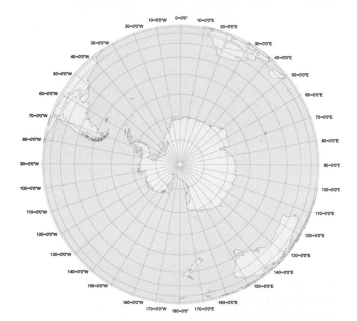

Instead, your focal point is a polar perspective that puts Antarctica at the center of that map (see **Fig. 3.6**). Maps, like any text, change according to our rhetorical situation, and the genres (and subgenres) we choose as authors help us reach our intended audiences more effectively.

Multimodal Genres: Defining the *What* and the *How*

When authors have a choice of what genre to produce for a project, sometimes the variety can seem overwhelming. At other times, the genre is mandated or seems self-evident. In a poetry-writing class, writing a poem is the expectation; in a biology class, writing a lab report is the expectation. In a business setting, if you respond to your supervisor's emailed question about the time of the meeting by printing a memo and putting it in her mailbox instead of sending a quick email reply, you've probably used the wrong genre and would send a totally wrong signal—one of passive aggression that may negatively impact your chances at that next promotion. Choosing the correct genre as an author shows that you understand the rhetorical situation and how to persuade and communicate with your audience. In this section, we provide some examples of genre types that new multimodal authors might find useful.

Static and Dynamic Genres

Static genres are genres we typically associate with analog presentations that are often found distributed in printed forms, such as posters, flyers, brochures, reports, paintings, and the like, but may equally appear in three-dimensional forms, such as statues, architectural models, rapid prototypes from 3-D printers, clothing, and other artifacts. We call these static genres because once they are produced for audiences they are meant to be read as a singular object, in one glance. That is, they don't move or change radically over time or with user interaction. **Dynamic genres**, on the other hand, do change and are often timeline based or require user interaction to work. Dynamic genres include videos, audio projects, websites, pop-up books, presentations, performances, and the like. In many cases, they are digital, like websites, but that's certainly not a requirement—pop-up books, for instance, have been a popular form of literature for both adults and children for nearly a millennium!

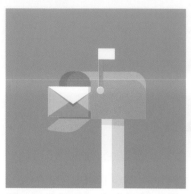

Figure 3.7 A Typical Mailbox Gif

Dacian G/Shutterstock

Like all genres, some change categories over time because they change genre conventions. For instance, a gif (graphics interchange format) is a digital genre created for use in the early days of the World Wide Web. Gifs used to be the predominant form of static image on the Web because of their small file size, which, in the early years of the Web, allowed for easy transmission over data lines that would only allow small bits of data to pass through at a time. Within a few years after the gif's creation, an animated option was created, which was generally used in ways unrelated to its original purpose. For instance, in the mid to late 1990s, the Web was filled with animated gifs of mailboxes opening and closing with a letter flying in to signal how to email the site author (see **Fig. 3.7**), or with Under Construction signs lighting up to show websites in progress. For expert users of the Web, these animated gifs were annoying at best.

Figure 3.8 Gifs in the News

In 2015, British television's Channel 4 launched a News Wall targeted at sixteen- to thirty-four-year-olds that consisted entirely of animated gifs.

Now, animated gifs are considered the *only* form of gif by most Web users, and these gifs include photographs strung together or a snippet of film on a loop with snappy captions to help tell the tale. Entire feature stories are told in gifs on some websites (see **Fig. 3.8**). So, the use of a genre all depends on the rhetorical situation: Are you designing a website for fourth-graders? Or university teachers? Is it 1997 or 2017? Is your site meant to be ironic or informational? As an author, knowing the context and purpose, along with your audience's tolerance for gifs (or any other genre), will go a long way in persuading them that you know what you're talking (or writing/designing) about.

Non/Linearity, Representation, and Association in Genres

In addition to authors choosing whether a static or dynamic genre is most suitable for their rhetorical situation, they can deepen meaning through their structural choices. Written text tends to persuade readers through a **linear** organization—we read one word after the other, forming meaning from words that build into sentences that build into paragraphs. We often make meaning from movies in the same way, watching one scene after another in a linear timeline.

Of course, both written text and movies can also be presented in **nonlinear** structures by their authors. This is what happens when we have flash-forwards and flashbacks in fiction and nonfiction stories, scripts, films, and other narrative genres. Nonlinearity adds a dynamic dimension to an otherwise linear or timeline-based text, and it thrives in multimodal texts as a meaning-making method. But it requires an audience that either expects, or can be taught to expect, this organizational pattern. The audience must then interact with the dynamic text to make sense of it as they piece together the chronology or identify the relationships between the parts and the whole. The Channel 4 News Wall in **Figure 3.8** (p. 68) presents a nonlinear organizational structure on the opening page, where readers can click anywhere they like to enter the text. Once inside the text, they are presented with linear news articles that may have additional linear or nonlinear multimodal elements, such as graphics, videos, or hyperlinks. One way readers can be taught to interpret these unexpected patterns is through the use of modes that draw on repetition, color, or other familiar design elements that help readers keep track of the persuasive purpose of the text.

Another method of designing a text that highlights its multimodality as a significant meaning-making technique is **representation.** Representation is *re*-presentation, or *re*-designing and *re*-communicating the purpose of a text through multimodal elements. For instance, if you're creating a text about eating habits in different cultures, maybe your text could look like a plate with different kinds of food on it. Your goal is to find a way of representing your topic that adds meaning to your text. This is called a *guiding metaphor*. Guiding metaphors add meaning to arguments by engaging multiple modes. For example, in the Case Study presented at the end of this chapter, Maria Andersen creates a guiding metaphor for her prezi: she uses an illustration of a game board to represent her argument that games promote learning. However, representations don't have to be visual. For instance, if you're working on an audio text, ask yourself whether it's useful for your sound effects to exactly mirror the narrative content—should the cat meow like a typical cat in your piece? Or does the cat represent something else — a lion, a ghost, a guardian angel—that might suggest a different sound effect?

As an author, if you're having trouble coming up with something that *represents* your idea, try brainstorming things that are *associated* with your idea instead. This strategy can be helpful if the representations you're coming up with seem too literal, too specific, or cliché (for example, if you're writing about love and the only representation you can come up with is a heart). **Association** uses an idea or concept related to your main purposes and uses a part of it to stand for a whole (also called *synechdoche*); in multimodal texts, a multimodal element can act as a simile for the whole text's purpose. Authors use association all the time in everyday texts. How often have you seen Mickey Mouse's ears used to mean the Disney Company, for example, or heard the term *9/11* used to refer to the September 11, 2001 terrorist attacks in the United States?

Elyse, a student of Kristin's, wanted to work on a Web-based portfolio that showcased her photography and videography skills. While she had little trouble composing the photo pages, she wanted to find a unique way to link to her short films. With Kristin, she brainstormed the various genres, such as trailers, through which filmmakers showcase their films. But, given the rhetorical situation of the assignment, Elyse didn't have time to make a trailer for each of her short films. She realized that movie posters would work better, since in a single glance a reader associates a movie poster as a stand-in to advertise a full-length movie. Elyse searched the Web for movie posters and began to compose posters for her films following the genre conventions (see **Fig. 3.9** for one example). Each poster linked to the film in her portfolio.

Figure 3.9 Movie Poster by Elyse Canfield

Elyse made this movie poster after brainstorming the best ways to visually link to her film projects on a portfolio website.

Elyse Canfield

◎— Touchpoint: Finding Your Genre

Like Elyse's example shows, it's important to find the right genre for your project. Sometimes the genre is defined for you—a stakeholder asks for a report, a documentary, a brochure, a flyer, a song, a memo. If that's the case, your job is a little easier than if you are presented with a scenario where you have to figure out which genre to use.

But let's say a client wants you to help him market his book, and that's all the instruction he knows to give you. In a case like this, you need to analyze the rhetorical situation of this book, as well as similar books, to figure out what genres will best help the readership of the book learn about it. You might compose flyers, a Twitter feed, a Facebook group, a press packet, or set up interviews and send out requests for book reviews. Sometimes multiple genres are needed to suit the situation, and part of whether you can do the work depends on your own skills in particular genres.

Recently, Cheryl worked with co-editor Drew Loewe to create a set of marketing materials for a book they wanted to promote: *Bad Ideas About Writing*.

The primary audience for the book was people who teach writing, or want to know how writing is taught, but who don't have research backgrounds in writing studies. This made publicity tricky because it was an unfamiliar audience. But they also wanted to reach readers who were academics and who attended an annual conference on writing studies where they could showcase some printed materials at an exhibit booth. So Drew designed a flyer that could mimic a possible book cover (see **Fig. 3.10**), and they provided a single proof copy of the book for display at the booth. To publicize that these materials were available at the conference, Cheryl circulated a selfie holding the proofs on her social media accounts (see **Fig. 3.11**) where she knew thousands of potential readers would see it. Sure enough, these two methods of multimodal outreach garnered attention for the book with the academic audience.

Figure 3.10 The Cover Flyer for *Bad Ideas About Writing*
Courtesy of Drew Loewe

Figure 3.11 A Selfie for Marketing Purposes
Courtesy of Cheryl Ball

But what should they have done to reach the nonacademic audience? What suggestions would you have made to them? Would you have circulated a video on Facebook or Twitter? Or are there other multimodal texts they could have made to promote the book?

What kind of project are *you* working on? How will you research the situation to understand the genres it will require? What genre(s) seem most likely to persuade audience you want to reach?

Genre Analysis: Analyzing the *What* and the *How*

Performing a genre analysis can pose the problem of COIK: Clear Only If Known—that is, how can a reader identify the genre of a text and relate it to other texts unless he or she is already familiar with that kind of genre to begin with? As teachers, we see this problem exhibited all the time when students call any printed form of a book a *novel* if they think it's read outside of an academic setting but call a book a *textbook* if it's any printed, long-form text read for a class. But they run into confusion when teachers mix genres, such as assigning a novel like Zadie Smith's *White Teeth* for a class but referring to it as a textbook. Artifacts can fall into multiple genres, or contain mixtures of genres, and conflating the genres of all printed, long-form books into either novels or textbooks—or just books—misses the nuances of these subgenres. A cookbook is not at all the same genre as a diary, which is again not at all the same genre as a biography. And those genres of books are totally different than self-help books, guides, or dictionaries, even though all of these examples are long-form, often-printed books.

And, yet, books are an easy example, relatively speaking, because they're so familiar. Most readers of *this* book (a guidebook, which is a subgenre of a textbook, for the record) will recognize it as a book, and maybe even a kind of textbook. Why? Because you recognize how its rhetorical and multimodal design elements—through words, layout, graphics, organizational structure, and so on—work together to form a whole, cohesive text. You've seen similar texts. You know that it is *not* a story in the narrative sense, so it's probably not a novel. And you are meant to learn explicit information from it. But how do you apply what you've implicitly learned about identifying genres, such as this textbook, to other kinds of multimodal texts?

Like a rhetorical analysis, which is meant to help readers and potential authors understand the audience, purpose, and context in which a text was designed (see Chapter 2), **genre analysis** is meant to help readers and potential authors examine how the container of that information allows the *what* (the content of your text) and the *how* (the form your text takes) to work together within specific rhetorical situations. In that way, genre analyses and rhetorical analyses work hand-in-hand; it isn't actually possible to separate what you want to say from how you will say it. Your topic and your design are closely connected, which is why this book is called *Writer/Designer*.

Figure 3.12 Panel from *Understanding Rhetoric*, by Elizabeth Losh, Jonathan Alexander, Kevin Cannon, and Zander Cannon

This panel talks about comics while using the genre conventions of a comic.

From *Understanding Rhetoric*, Second Edition, by Elizabeth Losh, Jonathan Alexander, Kevin Cannon, and Zander Cannon. ©2017, 2014 Bedford/St. Martin's, p. 17.

You can't be just a writer or just a designer; you're always both. And it's more useful to interpret how and why a particular genre works for a text if the reader knows the rhetorical situation in which the text is being used.

Analyzing Genre Conventions

Even if you're just posting an update to Twitter, you have to consider what you will say, how you will say it given who will see it, the context (the time of day, the event about which you're posting, etc.), and the ways that Twitter allows you to post supplementary information, such as links or photos. Additionally, the design of Twitter's user interface restricts the choices you can make as you craft your tweet; for example, you can't post anything longer than 140 characters. This situation is both rhetorical, in which you have to persuade a specific audience within a specific context, and generic, in that your purpose must be enacted within the confines of Twitter's conventions, some of which include the real-time nature of posting, the 140-character limit, the use of hashtags, occasional textspeak ("c u soon") to suit your audience or fit the character limit, and the integration of multimedia, as necessary. All of those characteristic features of Twitter posts are **genre conventions**.

Figure 3.13 Genre Conventions of Twitter

In this selection of tweets, Kristin employs genre conventions of tweets such as (top) a retweet with a personal note pointing followers to author Roxane Gay's interview; (middle) a funny but otherwise plain ol' tweet about Kristin's day that fits within the 140-character constraints; and (bottom) a tweet that also fits within the 140-character limit while employing txtspeak, a conference hashtag, a tan-skinned high-five emoji, and a call out to @thaigirl4, who was in charge of the conference.

If you learn to analyze the genre conventions of multimodal genres, you can better understand a text's rhetorical situation and apply that analytical skill to any kind of text you come across. You can also add more design choices to your rhetorical knowledge every time you compose a text for a new rhetorical situation.

For example, if you were to analyze breast cancer pamphlets, you would find that almost all of them feature a pink ribbon and a script-like font. These are genre conventions that authors and readers use to make meaning within a rhetorical situation because they are design elements that have become socially accepted as a metaphorical representation of breast cancer. It's important to analyze how conventions are used within texts because genre conventions are a good starting place when designing a similar text for a similar rhetorical situation. They help us understand what audiences expect from particular kinds of texts in particular kinds of situations. For example, if you're making a breast cancer awareness brochure, do you need to use the pink ribbon in order to be taken seriously? Or are there good reasons to break with this genre convention? As we saw with the figure of the lemons in Chapter 2 (see p. 40), just because a design element like the pink ribbon has become part of the social fabric of a particular genre and rhetorical situation doesn't mean that it's the only design element possible; sometimes changing that element can help a designer reach a whole new audience.

Questions for Genre Analysis

When analyzing genre, the following questions help you discover patterns that illuminate genre conventions across multiple sets of texts in a single genre:

- How is the text written and designed? How does a text convey its meaning? What modes and media does it predominantly use? Is it similar to other texts you've seen? How so?

- How are these multimodal elements organized in the text? Do they create hierarchies of emphasis? spatial relationships? navigational choices appropriate to the situation?

- Does the text contain a combination of other genres? How does the mixture of genres work together to convey meaning?

- How might you define the genre (or subgenres) of the text? If it is a subgenre, what conventions are different from its main genre that make it seem different?

- What is the purpose of this particular genre in relation to this particular rhetorical situation? What does the genre expect from readers? What does it allow/ask readers to do?

⊚— Touchpoint: Analyzing Musical Genres

What are the conventions of songs that can be classified under the genres of rock, pop, jazz, classical, rap, disco, or country? Some classical music, with its soothing stringed instruments or mellow piano solos, might help relax or calm us, while disco's quick, pulsing beats and high-hat taps might energize us enough to dance. Sites such as Google Play and Spotify categorize songs by musical genres and suggest certain playlists in genres depending on the listener's mood, which he or she can pick from using an interactive mood list that may also incorporate images (see **Fig. 3.14**). These tools—and our brains—rely on pattern recognition to classify musical genres. That pattern recognition is based on genre conventions. And while not every song within a particular genre uses the exact same conventions, being able to recognize the patterns can help us distinguish one song, and genre, from another.

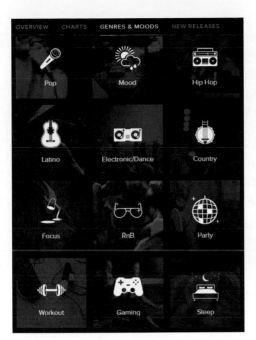

Pick a song, any song—it may be your favorite song, your most hated song, the most popular song on the radio, the song you're listening to right now. What mood does it put you in? What patterns does it have? How is it structured? Are the answers to these questions related? Identify and consider other songs in the same genre: Do they make you feel the same way? Do they have similar patterns or structures? How would you answer the Questions for Genre Analysis from page 76 for your genre?

Figure 3.14 Spotify Playlists

Streaming services like Spotify help listeners choose a musical genre and song based on mood or activity.

CASE STUDY

Analyzing Multimodal Genres in Game Studies

Two Different Genres: The *What* versus the *How*

Let's look at two examples to see more clearly how genres are dependent on the connection of the *what* and the *how* and on the rhetorical situation. Here are two texts that discuss the topic of video games and learning:

1. A scholarly book called *What Video Games Have to Teach Us about Learning and Literacy* by James Paul Gee, in which the author, drawing on lots of other scholarly research, argues that video games help promote literacy because they offer complicated, interactive narratives that game players have to learn to navigate. (See **Fig. 3.15**.)

2. A prezi (an interactive, online, multimedia presentation application) called "Playing to Learn?" by Maria Andersen, in which she argues that using

games in the classroom is an effective teaching tool because it engages students' brains in different ways and keeps them interested in learning tough topics (like math, which she teaches). (See **Fig. 3.16**.)

So the *what* is that these two scholar-teachers agree that games are good pedagogical tools. And they give lots of scholarly and popular examples as to why games are good for us. In making our own project, we could cite either of these texts to support our own argument about games. Citing sources is something you probably have some experience with already (see Chapter 6 for more info on citation), so for now we want to focus on *how* these authors make their arguments.

On the one hand, Gee (pronounced like the letter G or "Gee whiz!") has written a scholarly book that relies on the genre's conventions (like prose, citations, and formal language) to connect with his audience. There are visual modes—a few tables—but the text consists mostly of words format-ted in a way that we're used to seeing in scholarly (or even popular) books. That is to say, his book looks pretty much like every other book in that genre (see **Fig. 3.15**).

146   ◖◗ What Video Games Have to Teach Us ◖◗

players make real people, such as their friends, into virtual characters in the game), they may come to realize at a conscious level certain values and perspectives they have heretofore taken for granted and now wish to reflect on and question.

This chapter is about the ways in which content in video games either reinforces or challenges players' taken-for-granted perspectives on the world. This is an area where the future potential of video games is perhaps even more significant than their current instantiations. It is also an area where we enter a realm of great controversy, controversy that will get even more intense as video games come to realize their full potential, for good or ill, for realizing worlds and identities.

SONIC THE HEDGEHOG AND CULTURAL MODELS

Sonic the Hedgehog—a small, blue, cute hedgehog—is surely the world's fastest, most arrogant, and most famous hedgehog. Originally Sonic was the hero in a set of games released by Sega, beginning in 1991 with the release of *Sonic the Hedgehog* on the Sega Mega Drive/Genesis, and then later games on the Sega Dreamcast. However, after the Dreamcast was discontinued, he showed up on the Nintendo GameCube in the game *Sonic Adventure 2 Battle* and on a number of other games platforms, as well (e.g., *Sonic and the Secret Rings* on the Nintendo Wii or *Shadow the Hedgehog* on the Nintendo Wii, the Sony PS2, and the Microsoft Xbox 360). Sonic can run really, really fast. He can go even faster—like a blurry blue bomb—when he rolls into a ball. Either way, he can race around and through obstacles, dash into enemies, and streak through the landscape, leaping high in the air over walls and barriers.

Figure 3.15 A Page from James Paul Gee's *What Video Games Have to Teach Us About Learning and Literacy*

Looks like a book, eh?

Figure 3.16 "Playing to Learn?," Maria Andersen's Prezi about Using Games to Teach Effectively

Looks like a game, eh?

Maria Andersen, Prezi, inc.

Andersen, on the other hand, has chosen to present the same topic using a much different design: a media-rich, interactive presentation on the website Prezi.com. She also includes citations and examples, just like Gee does, although hers are usually much more brief because of the design conventions afforded by the Prezi interface. (We'll talk more in Chapter 7 about the impact of technological choices on designing multimodal projects.) However, unlike Gee, Andersen makes her argument about how games promote learning by designing her text to *look like* a game (see **Fig. 3.16**), which adds visual, spatial, and gestural meaning to her linguistic text. Andersen doesn't have to present as much linear, written information as Gee does to get a similar point across because she has the visual, spatial, and gestural design of the text do some of that work better than the linguistic mode could do. Thus, *how* Gee and Andersen present their topics is as important as *what* they want readers to get from their texts.

Gee's and Andersen's works are different, despite their similar topics, because they are written for different audiences and purposes. Gee's purpose is to reach an audience of public readers who are interested in games and reading practices; he also wants to reach academics who study literacy and gaming. Andersen's purpose is to use the multimodal and interactive affordances of a prezi, which helps her create a gamelike experience, to persuade teachers that games can engage students' brains by keeping them interested in learning tough topics. One text is meant for solitary, in-depth reading, while the other could be presented to a group of people in a shorter amount of time. One text is not better than the other because they serve different rhetorical situations.

The Same Genre: Analyzing Conventions

Now, let's compare texts within the same genre: Andersen's gaming prezi with two other prezis about the same topic (see **Figs. 3.17** and **3.18**). We can use this exercise to figure out what genre conventions authors of prezis have come to use and have used successfully.

Prezi software is based on our genre knowledge of other presentation tools (like Keynote and PowerPoint, which are in turn based on our knowledge of poster presentations). However, Prezi is also significantly different from other presentation software in that it allows readers to create zooming and animation features that are very difficult, if not impossible, to use in other presentation tools. For this reason, it is rare to run across a PowerPoint presentation that you're expected to interpret without any help from the author (e.g., notes posted online from a class lecture are still intended to go *with* the face-to-face lecture), whereas with Prezi you are more likely to run across presentations that stand on their own. Thus, similarity across prezis

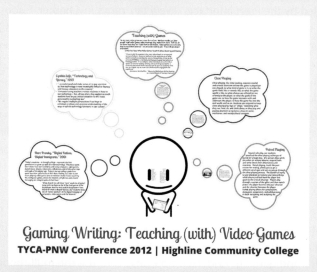

Figure 3.17 Visual Outline for Edmond Chang's "Gaming Writing: Teaching (with) Video Games"

Courtesy of Edmond Chang

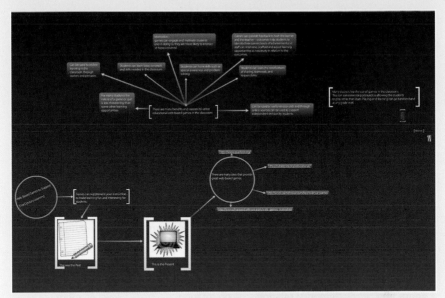

Figure 3.18 Visual Outline for William Maelia's "Using Web-Based Games to Support 21st Century Learning"

William Maelia, Prezi, Inc.

becomes one possible genre convention, as noted in the table on page 82 (on the row titled "Does the text make sense on its own?"). We could list many more conventions in the table, but we'll leave it at these, just to give you an idea of how you might come up with your own comparative list. For example, based on the number of readers who have "liked" each of the prezis in the table, we might be able to judge the prezis' relative success, although such an evaluation doesn't do justice to some of the successful qualities within the two prezis that have few or zero likes so far. The more stand-alone the prezi is, the more successful it seems to be.

Of course, if you are required to create a presentation for your multimodal project and you know that the rhetorical situation requires you to deliver it personally, perhaps your presentation will still be successful even if your prezi doesn't stand alone. You just have to figure out *which* conventions are needed to make the text interesting and useful for your audience. For instance, the three prezis analyzed here use the standard linear navigation path, which allows readers to click on the right arrow to navigate to the next set of information, as opposed to readers skipping around or the authors placing information outside of the path for readers to discover on their own. The latter types of navigation would be more appropriate for readers to play with in a stand-alone piece than in a public presentation. The navigation path that your presentation uses is a design decision you have to make based on your rhetorical situation.

Prezi Genre Conventions

Prezis	Andersen's "Playing to Learn?"	Chang's "Gaming Writing: Teaching (with) Video Games"	Maelia's "Using Web-Based Games to Support 21st Century Learning"
URL (for reference)	http://prezi.com /rj_b-gw3u8xl/	http://prezi.com /ai6wnm0l_j1l/	http://prezi.com /yiknhf2wapi_/
Background color	White	White	Blue
Navigation	Left and right arrows	Left and right arrows	Left and right arrows
Use of words	Uses titles, quotes, and explanatory text	Uses titles, quotes, and explanatory text	Uses titles and explanatory text
Levels of zoom and rotation	Zooms in on key elements; rotation follows game board path	Zooms in on frame; no rotation	Mostly uses same level of zoom throughout (with a few variances); minimal rotation
Author	Bio and contact info in Prezi	Contact info in Prezi	No information in Prezi
Use of images	Images supplement the written text	Images convey an example	Very few images are used, and mostly for shock value
Path points	120	14	20
Does the text make sense on its own?	Yes	Yes	Yes
Use/purpose of navigational path	Path is designed around a background illustration that corresponds to the argument; great "bigger picture" view	Path revolves around central figure; "bigger picture" conveyed through thought bubbles	Path is based on mind-mapping concept, but not all nodes are related; some "bigger picture" purpose
Citations	Yes	Yes	No (but there is a resource list)
Number of reader likes	More than 2,200	< 10	0
Use of video/ animation	Yes (15)	No (0)	No (0)

What if the Genre Is Unclear?

When researching texts for your multimodal project, you may come across a text whose genre is unclear. If you don't know the genre of a text, remember that genres are created based on other genres, on shared social circumstances, and for rhetorical situations that authors are familiar with. So, if you don't know the genre, ask yourself what the text *reminds* you of. Then maybe ask a few of your friends, your supervisor, or your teacher the same question. It's likely that collectively you'll be able to identify a genre that most closely fits the kind you want to study further. Also, texts sometimes mash up multiple genres. For example, when social networking sites (like Twitter) were first created, they asked users to "microblog" in 140 characters or less, whereas blog posts are typically much longer than that. The term *microblog* shows that when status updates were new, they were compared most closely in genre to blogs. So if you encounter a text whose genre is new to you, see what other genres the text relates to and consider studying those as well.

write/design! assignment

Analyzing Genre Conventions for Your Project

Now it's time for you to start working on your multimodal project, putting together your skills in rhetorical-multimodal-genre analysis. This step assumes that you have a project concept in mind—one that a client or supervisor has provided or one that you have artistic freedom to create yourself. If you don't yet have a multimodal project in mind, you can use the example proposal from Chapter 4 or a project you've worked on in any of the Touchpoint activities, talk to your teacher or supervisor for ideas, or just pick your favorite kind of text to practice with.

1. Find and read eight to ten texts across a range of media. They should all be on the same topic, as with "game studies" in the Case Study above.

2. List the arguments, points, or key ideas those texts offer about your topic. This is the *what*. For instance, in the Case Study above, both Gee and Andersen chose to focus on how teaching games improves students' learning. That's a key idea within the topic of games.

3. Next, list the multimodal design choices (think back to the list of modes in Chapter 1—linguistic, visual, aural, spatial, and gestural—and the design choices in Chapter 2—emphasis, contrast, organization, alignment, and proximity) that the texts use. This is the *how*.

4. Analyze the relationship between the *what* and the *how* (using rhetorical genre analysis—context, author, purpose, audience, and genre) and decide which texts seem the most successful given their rhetorical situations.

5. Identify which themes in those successful texts most inspire you to do further research. (If a key idea seems to be missing from the list you compiled in step 2, that might also be a good place to do more research.) Shorten your list of themes down to one or two ideas.

6. Pick one genre from those texts that you think best fulfills the author's purposes for that rhetorical situation. Do some research to find two or three more texts in that genre (they do not have to be on the same topic, although they might be). If several genres seem particularly appealing and successful, research them all.

7. Analyze the examples in this genre or genres and make a list or table of similarities and differences. These might relate to design choices such as layout, navigation, and multimodal elements, as well as to what each of those choices accomplishes within the text. You may also list rhetorical choices such as audience, purpose, context, historical period, and so on. Refer to Chapter 2 for a sampling of rhetorical and design choices that you might use. Also, see the Case Study on pages 77–82 for an example of how to create this table.

   What design elements are similar? Do they look similar or function in a similar way across most of the examples? If so, you have a genre convention. Make a short list of all the conventions for that particular genre, which you should keep as a handy checklist when designing and assessing the quality of your own multimodal project in that same genre.

write/design! option: Infographics as Visual-Argument Genres

One interesting place to see multimodal rhetorics at work is in the increasingly common genre of infographics like the one on page 85. The multiple modes available for use in infographics give writer/designers a set of affordances with the potential to make information more appealing, accessible, and inviting to a larger audience through placing those ideas within a story.

A writer/designer creating an infographic has to make rhetorical and multimodal choices to best fit her audience, purpose, and context. One of the cardinal rules of an infographic is to keep it concise, stripping away everything except the essentials. At the same time, every element, from font style, size, and color to the use of photographs, charts, and graphs has an impact on how an audience will make sense of information and respond to an infographic's message.

Begin by selecting a topic or issue of interest to you or that is suggested by your instructor. Search for and save at least five infographics on your topic. As you begin collecting your infographic examples, consider the following questions and be ready to discuss them with the rest of the class:

- Which infographic is your favorite and why? Which is your least favorite and why?
- Which infographic do you think is the most informative and why? Is it also the most persuasive one? Why or why not?

- Which mode, media, and design choices seem to make the most sense for the subject and context? Are these used in the same way in all five examples or do they work particularly well in just one?

Once you've chosen your topic and done a quick genre analysis of other infographics on the subject, it's time to start composing your own. Your purpose is to condense and visualize your topic/research material, making it more comprehensible and persuasive for a broad audience.

While you can always create an infographic by hand, drawing on a large piece of paper, you might also want to do a first or final draft digitally. There are many free or low-cost options for creating your own infographic online. Sites such as Piktochart, Infogr.am, Easeily, or Visme have a set of free templates or the option to join with access to dozens more templates. Just make sure to check how these sites allow you to access your infographic after you create it, in case you need to send a copy to your teacher or client—not all allow you to download your text after you've made it. Alternatively, you can search online for infographic templates.

Building Tips

Tell a story
Put your information in context and help your audience see the big picture

Clear the clutter
Strip out unnecessary details and include only essentials

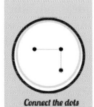

Connect the dots
Help your audience understand your argument and why it matters

Use images
Photos, graphs, & other images convey lots of information in little space

Use size and color
These elements will help to emphasize your most important details

Remember your audience
Prioritize communication and persuasion over making it beautiful

Figure 3.19 Visual Arguments Infographic

Infographic writer/designers have to balance ways of making their texts visually appealing and informative with the need to communicate ideas, data, and arguments clearly, concisely, and persuasively. This infographic is about creating infographics (meta!). The steps are clearly arranged, and visuals make the text appealing while conveying information through symbols. The text is kept to a minimum, with clear, directive titles ("Tell a story") and brief elaboration in a less emphatic font.

Piktochart made by Jennifer Sheppard

4 How Do You Start a Multimodal Project?

So far in this book, we have discussed what multimodal texts are, how they work rhetorically through design, and the role that genre plays in communicating an author's message to an audience. Since the point of this book is to help you become a multimodal writer/designer, we now want to offer a big-picture perspective of how authors begin the process of making multimodal projects.

As you gain expertise at writing/designing, the process becomes easier, and you might even be able to skip some of these steps (or work them out informally). These steps should not be taken as set in stone. They are guides for thinking through the composition process, not a rigid, lockstep method for getting things done.

This chapter provides an overview of the typical early stages of a multimodal composition process, including brainstorming and refining intial ideas, pitching those possibilities to others as a means of gaining feedback, researching, planning and articulating a more detailed proposal, and developing mode-appropriate drafts (e.g., storyboards, mock-ups, wireframes, and prototypes). We then demonstrate how that process can play out in more detail through a comprehensive Case Study. While the Case Study example is likely more complex than what you will be working on at this stage, we hope that showing you this process in full will help you determine how to proceed on your own multimodal projects, now and in the future. The Write/Design! assignment that concludes the chapter guides you through proposing a project of your own and drafting a realistic timeline. Chapter 5, How Do You Design and Revise with Multiple Audiences?, will show you the rest of the process, from revision to finished product.

What Are You Supposed to Produce?

Persuasive texts are almost always written in response to some situation. Sometimes the authors producing those texts are self-motivated to action, such as writing a letter to the editor of a newspaper about a local issue the author is passionate about. When they aren't self-motivated, projects are the result of someone else giving instructions to follow: a teacher giving an assignment, a supervisor delegating a task to an employee, a citizen organization requesting a meeting with a government official to discuss a local community issue, a research group sending out a Request for Proposals (RFP), an organization soliciting business through an advertisement, an owner of a lost pet posting a flyer, and so on. Each of these projects presents a new rhetorical situation that requires analysis to determine the purpose and audience(s), as well as the genre needed to fulfill the stakeholders' expectations.

This is where the analytical skills you built up in Chapters 2 and 3 will be useful for designing your own multimodal project. Determining what you are supposed to produce, for whom, for display in which genre, and by when is the first step in figuring out how you will complete your multimodal project. Once you've arrived at some initial answers to these questions, you are ready to begin drafting your project. Just remember, even the best laid plans need adjustments, so build in at least a little flexibility.

Brainstorming Your Project Ideas

A big part of designing is experimenting with ways of combining content and form. This means that there isn't one perfect way to begin and it's perfectly OK (and normal) for your first ideas to need refinement. Coming up with several ideas as you conceptualize your project is a good strategy because sometimes your first idea might be too literal or clichéd, or it just may not be what you want. Once you have a general idea of your overall project and purpose, you can experiment to flesh out some of the details about what works and what doesn't. While this trial-and-error process can often take a long time initially, it's good practice to analyze multiple modes in relationship to one another and often helps you develop unexpected communication possibilities. Plus, the more you practice putting modes together and analyzing how they affect readers, the more quickly you'll be able to design your next multimodal project.

Begin by brainstorming some design ideas. Record them quickly. It's not about how well you can draw or write but rather about getting the ideas down in visual and spatial (not just linguistic) form. It's also important that you don't censor yourself or stop to judge your ideas at this stage. You can evaluate them later because now is the time for generating possibilities.

Figure 4.1 Cheryl's Visual Design Brainstorming

Cheryl's drawing visualizes the basic design of a collaborative webtext that she worked on and that was later published in an online journal.

Courtesy of Cheryl Ball

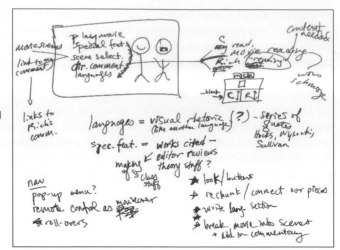

As Cheryl's visual brainstorming example illustrates in **Figure 4.1**, this part of the composing process isn't about making things look pretty but rather about visualizing and recording your initial ideas. We recommend you choose a brainstorming format that seems most comfortable and intuitive to you and then get started! You could draw simple stick figures, make flowcharts, use icons to represent certain kinds of content, use colored pencils or crayons if color is a significant part of the visual design, or work with other "craft" materials that you feel comfortable playing with as you experiment: scissors, modeling clay, stickers, and so on. Your brainstorming doesn't need to be elaborate—and, in fact, *shouldn't* be elaborate at this stage. Focus on speed and quantity of ideas, not quality. There will be time later to perfect them. And although some authors are more adept at creating these visualizations on their computers, we find that most authors are better off using pen and paper because it's less of an initial commitment and provides a quicker way to brainstorm.

⊚— Touchpoint: Multimodal Brainstorming

Imagine that your intramural soccer club has asked you to design a flyer to recruit more players for the upcoming season that starts next semester. Your club has decided to post the flyer in the residence halls and the student fitness center to target students new to campus and those who already enjoy physical activity. It is particularly important to recruit women players, as the team needs to have a certain ratio of men to women to qualify for the league. Given this rhetorical situation, brainstorm some initial design ideas for the flyer. Consider the following questions as you work:

- Your genre has already been designated as a flyer, but what are the options and conventions within the genre that would best suit your needs (paper size, type of paper, layout, those little tear-away tags at the bottom so that your audience physically takes a copy of your club's contact information)?

- What basic information must be included (game and practice times, season duration, costs, field locations, etc.)?

- What design elements and participation perks can you emphasize to encourage students to join? What specific strategies will you use to recruit women players?

- What design constraints do you have to work with (team or school colors, logos, images, etc.)?

Pitching Your Project

Once you have done some brainstorming and reflected on the kind of project you plan to make, your next step is to refine those early ideas so that you can seek feedback from others and move forward with developing your initial draft. Since there is no single approach or kind of text that will work in all situations for all audiences, knowing how to perform rhetorical analyses and looking closely for genre conventions will help you figure out how to write or design any kind of text. However, it's also important to look for guidance and insight from others to see if there are alternative perspectives or approaches you need to incorporate. By explaining your early project ideas to your teacher, boss, client, or stakeholders before you begin the bulk of your design work, you can be better assured that you're on the right track as you create a text for a particular rhetorical situation.

A **pitch** is a short and informal presentation or write-up that briefly conveys your initial project concept. It explains how the *what* (content) and the *how* (form) of your idea might come together in the final project. It's a means of convincing audience members who have some stake in what you are proposing that you understand the situation/issue, have an interesting and relevant plan for approaching it, and can successfully accomplish the project at hand. (Pitches are sometimes called elevator speeches, drawing on the idea of a writer who is on an elevator with a publisher and has only a few floors to convince the publisher to accept his or her book proposal.) Importantly, pitches can also be used as way of getting feedback on the concept and direction of your project *before* you have spent time developing it. Once you've gotten support or approval for an idea you've pitched, you can start fleshing out the form and content of the project in the recursive stages discussed later in this chapter.

Keep in mind that at this point you have not completed a lot of research into the topic or designs, so there will be room for change. This is the same basic process used in writing essays; you have an intial idea based on the assignment directions, but as you begin researching and writing on the topic your focus might become more concrete, or it might change direction, or it might even take a completely different form.

A pitch (or a more formal proposal, discussed at the end of this chapter) can be especially valuable for writer/designers of multimodal texts. That's because a change in topic or a refinement in your argument might cause a significant rethinking and reworking of the project's genre, design, and use of multiple modalities—it's no longer as easy as cutting and pasting words into a different order. You should expect and plan for some level of contingency in your project idea as your work progresses, but the more you can work out the kinks through a pitch or proposal before drafting, the more efficient your efforts will be.

Designing Your Pitch

Once you've brainstormed your ideas, it's time to put together a pitch for your instructor, supervisor, peers, or other stakeholders. (Note that sometimes you will create a pitch or a proposal, not both. While each is a useful kind of planning tool, these texts can also differ in timing, scope, audience, research, and level of detail.) When planning your pitch, make sure you address the following details about your project:

- What is the rhetorical situation for your multimodal project (as opposed to your pitch)?
- What is your topic?
- What genre will you use for your project?
- How will you design your project in relation to your topic? How is the design appropriate to your project's rhetorical situation? Providing drawings from a multimodal brainstorm session (like the ones you may have done for the Multimodal Brainstorming Touchpoint on pp. 88–89) might be useful here.

- What do you need to know or learn so that you can complete your project? (In other words, how do you convince your instructor or client that you are able to complete this project in the time frame given?)

You'll also need to think about designing the pitch itself:

- What is the rhetorical situation of your pitch?

- What genre of pitch does the rhetorical situation require (live presentation, stand-alone presentation, paper handouts, a formal written proposal)?

- What are the genre conventions you will use to pitch your project?

- How will you convey your topic to your pitch audience? How much do they need to know at this point in the project, and what will you tell them to hook their interest? (How much more research do you need to do?)

- Are there other requirements for your pitch, such as a time limit, a specific technology, or a dress code?

Figure 4.2 (p. 92) illustrates how one student used these guidelines to pitch her project for improving access to lactation rooms on campus. After brainstorming and then writing up her ideas, Sarah pitched her project to her instructor and classmates, who then asked questions and offered suggestions to refine her plans.

◉— Touchpoint: **Putting a Project Pitch into Action**

Consider a multimodal project you've seen or are working on. Or, if you aren't currently working on a project, imagine you're developing a novel or movie idea and you need to pitch the idea to a publisher or film studio (stakeholders) so that they invest in your project. Using the questions for designing your pitch on pages 90–91 as a guide, consider the elements you need to address as you write/design your pitch.

- What is the rhetorical situation and genre for the project?

- What is your topic, and what research do you need to do?

- How will you design your pitch? You could use a simple pitch like Sarah did (see **Fig. 4.2**) or you might decide to use another medium or genre such as a video pitch.

Once you have considered these questions, create your pitch! Then practice it with your co-workers, classmates, or friends before pitching it to your stakeholders.

Improving Access to Lactation Rooms on Campus

Sarah

My idea for the project is to integrate my internship at the Women's Resource Center with advocacy for expanded lactation room locations on campus. This is a critical issue because with 35,000 students at this university, there is a large population of students, faculty, and staff who are moms and very few resources are provided to support their success. Right now, there are only three lactation rooms on campus: one in the Women's Resource Center, one in the library, and one inside of the student union. There are currently about 30 women who are actively involved in the lactation program, but there is a lack of both space and ease of access. All lactation room users have to schedule an appointment in advance to take care of their needs. This is a problem because, biologically, women may need to express milk at varying times that can't be planned in advance. In addition to the scheduling issues, the physical locations of the existing rooms and the large geographic footprint of our campus can force users to walk 15-20 minutes one-way to access one of the rooms. This can obviously negatively affect the work, retention, and academic/professional success of the mothers of our campus community.

35,000 students on campus

3 lactation rooms

My project will advocate for three primary changes.

1
More Rooms
The program needs to obtain additional lactation room spaces across campus so that they are more easily accessible.

2
Flexible Scheduling
A more flexible scheduling system should be developed so that moms can find an available room on an as-needed basis.

3
Improved Equipment
All new and existing lactation rooms should be equipped with necessary items (breast pumps, wipes, etc.) needed by lactating mothers.

In order to achieve this plan, I propose to work closely with the coordinator at the Women's Resource Center to create a proposal and presentation to advocate for more rooms and supplies. My target audience for this project will be the Associated Students' student organization funding committee. The genre I plan to use is a slide presentation that includes cost charts, student population graphs, lactation room layouts, and other relevant images.

Figure 4.2 **A Student Pitch**
Sarah Tanori/Jennifer Sheppard

Drafting to Stakeholder Expectations

Once you have pitched your ideas and gotten approval from your target audience (or other stakeholders), it's time to start the drafting process. At this stage, your work will likely include conducting research on your project's issue or topic, outlining your project's structure, and getting your rough ideas into physical form on paper, screen, or other modality.

Drafting is a recursive process. That means that you will continually make new content and then work to revise it to better suit your audience, purpose, and genre, which may then cause you to do more research, and so on. Depending on which genre you are composing, drafting might mean producing a different kind of text at various stages of the drafting process: from sketches or brainstorms; to initial drafts, storyboards, and scripts; to pitches and proposals; to rough cuts and alpha versions; to polished rough drafts such as prototypes or models.

Which term you use depends on what medium you're working in: the terms *rough cut*, *storyboard*, and *script* tend to be used with timeline-based projects such as videos or audio texts. These forms of drafts allow you to plot out the linear order of content and what it will contain. In contrast, *prototype*, *wireframe*, *alpha version*, and *mock-up* are drafting terms typically used with code-based projects such as websites, apps, and software programs. As you'll see in the Case Study later in this chapter, mock-ups and prototypes are often visual representations of how a project will look, but they don't yet contain any functionality to make them work. Further, keep in mind that different types of drafts are used for different purposes, with earlier options usually reserved for helping an author get his or her thoughts together on a project and later versions used for feedback from colleagues, clients, and occasionally target audiences themselves to fine-tune the final version.

Figure 4.3 Rough Cut of a Frog Sculpture

Biosphoto/Superstock

Part Two of *Writer/Designer* provides an in-depth look at each of these forms of drafting, depending on what your composing needs are, so be sure to see these sections to select a genre appropriate for drafting your multimodal text:

- Outlines (pp. 183–84)
- Sketches (pp. 184–85)
- Models (pp. 185–86)
- Wireframes (pp. 187–89)
- Mock-Ups (pp. 189–91)
- Storyboards (pp. 191–94)
- Scripts (pp. 194–95)
- Rough Cuts (pp. 195–96)

Figure 4.4 The Stages of Drafting, Frog-Style
Biosphoto/Superstock

◎— Touchpoint: **Choosing a Draft Genre**

After reading the information in this Drafting to Stakeholder Expectations section, visit the detailed drafting sections in Chapter 7, pages 181–96. Consider a project you are working on, the rhetorical situation, and your goals. Which genre is the right one for your project draft? Why is it the best choice?

Choose one and begin drafting your project!

Using the Feedback Loop

Authors rarely work in a vacuum with no feedback from an instructor, boss, or other stakeholder, and writing/designing multimodal projects is no exception. When you draft a multimodal project for an audience, it's a good idea to solicit feedback from them that you can incorporate into your text. The **feedback loop** is a method for checking your work with your stakeholders (see also the Chapter 5 sections on peer review on pages 120–27). Feedback can happen throughout the process and often results in multiple revisions. This process is rarely linear and is often referred to as a loop. That is, you share your project, receive feedback, make revisions and move forward, and then receive more feedback, continuing on until you and/or the stakeholders (ideally both!) are satisfied.

You can also participate in others' feedback loops: your fellow students or colleagues will often ask you to give them feedback on their early work. Providing productive feedback to others not only helps them but also strengthens your own critical skills and might even trigger ideas for your own work.

Besides classroom peer review, you may be familiar with other names for the feedback loop process, such as *workshopping* or *usability*

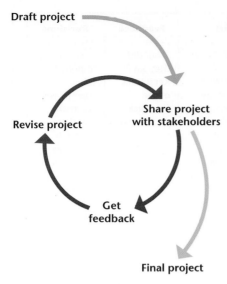

Figure 4.5 The Feedback Loop

testing. Typically, workshops are a part of the process that happens within a writing class and are a valuable part of the writing, design, and revision process. But since this book focuses on both real-world and classroom projects, our feedback loop is similar to usability testing, a term you hear in technical communication and other professional circles. Usability testing asks real users—those people who are the target audience of your project—to perform certain tasks with your materials and report on their experiences. Since we suspect that users of this book are somewhere between the writing classroom and the professional world (if not in both), we use *feedback loop* as a compromise.

Finding out what your audience sees at this stage will forecast whether your design draft will successfully match what they want, need, and expect from the finished project. If your current plan isn't working, the feedback you receive should help you make changes to the draft and present it again until the draft is on the right track for its rhetorical situation. You don't want to progress too far along in composing the full project itself if you're not sure it will suit the rhetorical situation. It's *much* easier to change a mock-up, storyboard, or other early draft than to change a finished multimodal project, so take advantage of your feedback loop.

⊚— Touchpoint: Tracking Your Feedback

Feedback comes at multiple stages in the composing process—after designing a pitch, creating a draft, presenting a formal proposal, or sometimes anywhere along that windy path. It's important to keep track of who your audience or stakeholders are and how they respond or buy in to your project. To identify and track your feedback loop, make a chart with the following columns, and add as many rows as you need. Keep in mind that this chart may grow and change as your project adapts. Add to this chart each time you get feedback on your project, including when you conduct a formal peer review (see Chapter 5, pp. 124–27, on Peer Reviewing Multimodal Projects).

Audience/ Stakeholder	Stage	Draft	Feedback	Revisions
Who are they? What are their roles? Does their feedback have more weight than someone else's might?	*When?* At what stage(s) of the process do you need to seek this feedback? You may need to return to certain people multiple times.	*What* kind of draft should you show this stakeholder? Do they require a certain format or would they respond best to a particular medium? How will you deliver the project to them? (See Chapter 7, Drafting Your Project, pp. 181–82 for ideas.)	*What* did they say? Keep track of the feedback you receive.	*How* will you respond? What changes will you make based on this feedback? (See Chapter 5, pp. 134–35 on Creating a Revision Plan.)

Designing for Your Primary Audience

As you'll see in the Case Study in this chapter, one team worked to meet the needs of their primary audience: family members visiting a museum together. Only by effectively analyzing the rhetorical situation of the museum's call for proposals—thereby understanding the main context, purpose, and audience of the client's project—could the team propose to build the right app for the primary audience. Determining the details of who will see, hear, and use your project, either as part of pitching your project and writing your proposal or as part of the asset-gathering stages, will make your project more focused and your design tactics more concise. (Details for gathering and tracking assets are discussed in more detail in Chapter 6.)

CASE STUDY

Pitching an App for the National Gallery

In this Case Study, we present a series of documents from a multimodal project to show how the authors moved from **brainstorming** and **conception** of their design idea to **drafting** and **prototyping**, including how they used the **feedback loop** to pitch the project back to the client. Although this Case Study is probably more complicated than what you will be writing/ designing at this stage, we hope that showing you this process in full will help you make conscious and productive decisions about how to proceed on your own multimodal project. Some parts of the analysis provided here (particularly in the Drafting a Prototype section) were adapted from the project documents, courtesy of Sarah Lowe, who was one of the instructors on this project.

The Rhetorical Situation

The project began when the Norwegian National Museum (NNM) (*audience*; *stakeholder*) published a solicitation (or call for ideas), asking designers (*authors*) to create activities (*text*) that would bring more museum patrons, especially families (*primary audience*), into some of their prominent, but less-visited, collections (*purpose*). As part of a joint US–Norwegian program in Museum Interaction Studies, two professors, Sarah Lowe and Palmyre Pierroux, along with their respective graphic design and education students, collaborated with the National Gallery in Oslo to pitch a set of interactive games, apps, and other activities (*genre*). In this Case Study, we present one student group's project, a game-like mobile app (*genre*) called Tales. The writer/designers on the team included Sofie Bastiansen, Kiernan Bensey, Mette Bergsund, August Houston, Heather McNamara, Alex Raykowitz, and Suzanne Rye (*authors*).

In order to complete this project, the team had to

- Read the solicitation and understand the museum's project requirements (*rhetorical situation*; *genre*)
- Research the National Gallery to get a sense of the space and to choose which lesser-known collection they wanted to focus on. The solicitation

Figure 4.6 Designers (Left to Right): Kiernen Bensey, Alex Raykowitz, August Houston, Heather McNamara.

The project team included students Sofie Bastiansen, Kiernan Bensey, Mece Bergsund, August Houston, Heather McNamara, Alex Raykowitz, and Suzanne Rye. Faculty and museum participants included Sarah Lowe, University of Tennessee Knoxville; Dr. Palmyre Pierroux, University of Oslo; Per Bakke, National Museum of Art, Architecture and Design, Oslo, Norway; and Anne Qvale, National Museum of Art, Architecture and Design, Oslo, Norway.

Courtesy of Sarah Lowe.

specified that the project could not focus on rooms with well-recognized art, such as the Edvard Munch exhibit with his famous painting, *The Scream*. (*rhetorical situation*)

- Analyze the rhetorical situation of their chosen exhibit—in this case, using the content from the Collection Highlights exhibit in the National Gallery (*context*) to create a game (*purpose*) for multigenerational families (*audience*)

- Figure out the challenges, constraints, and other requirements that would be necessary to work with and against when designing their project (*modes*; *affordances*; *design elements*; *audience*; *purpose*; *context*)

- Ensure that the project met all the stakeholders' requirements, including primary audiences (families visiting the museum), secondary audiences (museum staff), and tertiary audiences (museum curators, designers, and investors) (*rhetorical situation*; *genre*; *audience*)

Researching the Rhetorical Situation for the Proposal

The group researched these aspects of the assignment by studying the museum, its layout, exhibits, and mission documents, talking with staff, and reading scholarly research about game theory and learning. In order to fully inform themselves about the rhetorical situation, they wrote up much of this research into a **design brief**, a genre of **proposals** used in the design field to spell out the research, planning, and design concepts of a multimodal project to persuade a client, audience, or other stakeholders that their proposed idea will accomplish the project's goals and is the best choice among a variety of options.

The Tales project team's design brief showcased their proposed project—a scavenger-hunt app—and demonstrated how this would be the best genre and approach to engage families with children, the target audience outlined in the NNM's solicitation. This design brief provided a summary of the research into the *who, what, when, where, why*, and *how* that the project team completed in order to create a text that would suit the NNM's rhetorical situation. The design brief itself is multimodal and designed to help the stakeholders (instructors, client, and audience) understand and visualize the project.

Each section of the design brief plays a necessary role in pitching the project, and we've included pieces of it here to help you see how the Tales team navigated all the elements we've covered in the previous chapters (rhetorical situation, design elements, modes, affordances, genre, etc.). The screenshots presented in the Case Study do not represent a real app. As we've discussed, designers commonly make sketches, mock-ups, and even videos of static objects and animate them so that they don't have to create a cumbersome, expensive prototype in the actual technology or medium of the final project. That's what the Tales team did here for their pitch and proposal.

(For more information about writing project **proposals** and **reports**, see pp. 107–8 the end of this chapter and Chapter 5, Reporting on Your Project, pp. 143–44.)

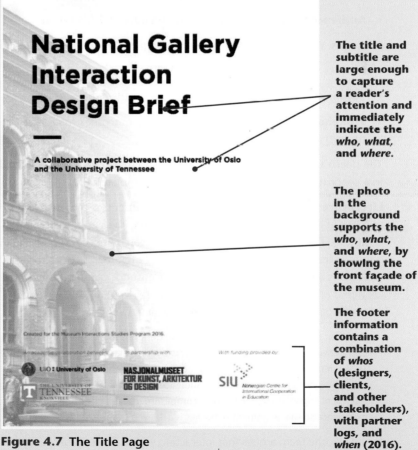

The title and subtitle are large enough to capture a reader's attention and immediately indicate the *who*, *what*, and *where*.

The photo in the background supports the *who*, *what*, and *where*, by showing the front façade of the museum.

The footer information contains a combination of *whos* (designers, clients, and other stakeholders), with partner logs, and *when* (2016).

Figure 4.7 The Title Page

Justification of Project

The first three sections of the proposal—Needs Analysis, Literature Review, and Competitive Analysis—provide background research summarizing the *why*, *what*, and *how*.

- **Needs Analysis (*Rhetorical Analysis*):** This focuses on the fundamentals of audience, purpose, and context (see Chapter 1). For instance, here's a list of the subheads within the team's Needs Analysis that indicate the individual needs the project team identified:

  - **Project partner:** Who is the National Museum? (*audience*; *context*)

  - **Content scope:** What exhibits would the game feature and why? (*purpose*)

  - **Audience:** What are families' needs and interests? (*audience*)

  - **Needs:** Why does the museum need to engage this audience? (*purpose*)

  - **Project Challenge:** What problem will our team solve? (*purpose*)

  - **Value:** What is the value of the outcome for the audience? (*purpose*)

  - **Stakeholders:** Who will be involved in the outcome? (*audience*; *context*)

  The needs analysis is similar to the background research you might include in a proposal for a project that has yet to be completed.

- **Literature Review (*Research*):** This section discusses the project's purpose in relation to previous research. For the Tales app, the team positioned their idea in conversation with research about using interactive games in learning environments. Lit reviews lend credibility (**ethos**) to your plans and help ensure that you aren't misunderstanding the rhetorical needs of a particular situation, or worse, reinventing the wheel. Here's a sample paragraph from the Literature Review overview:

  > Based on the literature, the intention of the design is to bridge this semantic gap between the museum and the visitors by facilitating a game-based activity. Through the game, the museum will be able to express [its] knowledge about the exhibitions and artworks to the audience. The value of a game is to facilitate a sense of engagement, feeling of accomplishment and … meaningful learning experience so that alignment of frames is achieved (Kapp, 2012).

  Essentially, the team argues that interacting with artwork through a game will give museum visitors greater insight into and appreciation of the pieces they engage with, and they cite educational theory to support this goal.

- **Competitive Analysis (*Genre Analysis*):** This section compares the proposed project's look, function, and genre to projects that have already been designed for similar rhetorical situations to evaluate what has worked, what hasn't, and what can be adapted or improved upon. (For more on genre analysis, see Chapter 3, pp. 73–82.) The Tales team reviewed five art apps similar to (or in competition with) the one they wanted to create. They summarized the research relevant to their own project:

   > When looking at these games and technologies as a collective, there are some important themes and concepts that become clear. In general, each one involves interaction between the technology or game and the audience making them more engaging [. . .] which, according to research, is how learning occurs. (17)

Competitive Analysis
Collection Highlights

ArtLens App (Gallery One)

The ArtLens app was designed for the Gallery One Art Exhibit within the Cleveland Museum of Art. This app allows you to experience the gallery space both within the museum and while at home, helping you to create a more personalized experience. At home, you are able to sort through the museum's gallery and view each piece as if you were there. When you are actually visiting the museum, you are able to walk around with the app through premade tours or simply scan them in order to see more information about each piece. You can then send your favorite pieces to the museum's Collection Wall that showcases images of the shared pieces.

Relevance:

An important aspect of this app is that it can exist beyond the walls of the museum, but in order to use it to its full potential, one must be within the space. It is important that our game be relevant within the space, but it may contain an aspect that can live outside of the museum.

12

Figure 4.8 The Competitive Analysis

This layout is typical in a report, which tends to privilege the use of images and summarized content that readers can quickly skim for meaning.

The image is emphasized according to its page placement and size because the visual design of the games are important to highlight in a competitive analysis.

A brief description fits into the remaining page length, with an informational header (the name of the app).

An even briefer paragraph indicates the relevance of analyzing this app.

Figure 4.9 Redd

The main character in the Tales app.

Courtesy of Sarah Lowe

Project Description

Based on the research they had conducted, the design team **brainstormed** ideas for this game-based app and settled on a scavenger-hunt genre that revolved around Redd, a red fox, who would help family members learn more about the artwork in the Collection Highlights section of the museum. Redd would ask them to work together to find clues that would help them solve the puzzle he presented. In choosing Redd, the team drew on local culture and the fact that foxes are curious scavengers, following trails and digging up clues. Thus, Redd's character is a metaphorical embodiment of the game's purpose. One of the team members, a graphic design student, drew a version of Redd that they could use to think about how the game might proceed (see **Fig. 4.9**).

The family works together to help Redd find all the objects he needs to overcome stage fright and sing and dance at the King's Banquet. Each family member uses a different set of age-appropriate questions in the app to locate the artwork. Once found, players get additional information through questions and facts about the artwork, and they are rewarded with a specific item from the painting that Redd needs. For example, upon successfully finding Pablo Picasso's painting *Guitare*, an abstract representation of a guitar, the family learns more about abstraction in art as a method for self-expression, then they receive the guitar that Redd will need when he performs for the King. The seek-and-find activity continues through several stops in the gallery, concluding with an animation of Redd performing at the King's Banquet.

Drafting and Designing the Prototype

To **draft** their project, the Tales app team drew some sketches on paper first, created a digital drawing of Redd that they could more easily add facial features and stances to, created a mock-up of the app interface in an image-manipulation program like Photoshop or Illustrator, and then placed those images onto pictures of smartphones to make it seem as if they had already designed the app (see **Figs. 4.10** and **4.11**). (There are more ideas in Chapter 7 on ways to create prototypes for different multimodal projects.)

Figure 4.10 The Game Begins

The fox's tail on the app's start screen points to the title of the game, Tales, which hearkens both to the tail of the fox and the narrative tale that the game provides. Each family member syncs their device to the code on the card, provided at the entrance to the museum exhibit. This initiates the game.

Courtesy of Sarah Lowe

In **Figure 4.11**, notice the repetition of color, design elements (Redd, the speech bubble, the "Found it!" button, navigational aids, etc.), and layout across the four screens. This design choice makes the different age-appropriate versions of the game feel like part of a single experience. The family plays as a team, with each of their player names at the top of each phone—but each player has a different set of clues appropriate for their age level. This design choice is based on the educational research the team has conducted on games and learning.

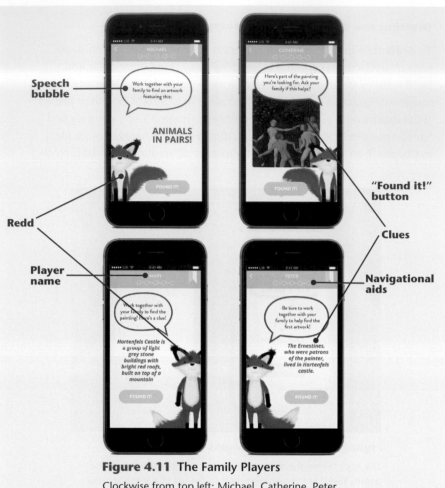

Speech bubble

Redd

Player name

"Found it!" button

Clues

Navigational aids

Figure 4.11 The Family Players

Clockwise from top left: Michael, Catherine, Peter, and Mary.

Courtesy of Sarah Lowe

Creating the Stakeholder Pitch

Earlier in the chapter (see pp. 89–92), we discussed how a **pitch** can be used to help audiences understand the *what*, *why*, and *how* of your initial project ideas. These pitches are often brief and leave lots of room for change in the project conception after getting feedback and doing more research, and often they occur before the formal proposal that presents research and justification for your project. But sometimes pitches, as in this case, are more like formal presentations, where you have a fairly fleshed-out version, including a prototype, of the actual project. In all pitches, your primary purpose is to persuade. You are trying to convince your audience of the value and relevance of your project ideas and why they should select yours over others.

With the design brief and prototype complete, the Tales team presented a very detailed pitch of the project to a set of stakeholders, which included their instructors and external design critics who could give them feedback before they gave their final presentation to the museum. In designing their pitch, the team had to consider how to present the full rhetorical situation of the museum project as well as what the internal and external critics might need to know, especially since some of those in the audience (like Cheryl) were hearing about the project for the first time. The entire thirty-minute presentation was fifty-five slides, with each slide having no more than a sentence or two of content or an image or series of related images.

One of the design team members started the presentation by immediately showcasing the purpose of the project with a slideshow designed to echo the design of the app prototype (see **Fig. 4.12**). To provide background on the project, they had to tell the audience, in brief, why they chose to do the project this way. They drew from the research in their design brief proposal to create slides that had short bits of written content, summarizing the longer analytical sections (see **Fig. 4.13**).

Figure 4.12 Pitch Title Slide
Courtesy of Sarah Lowe

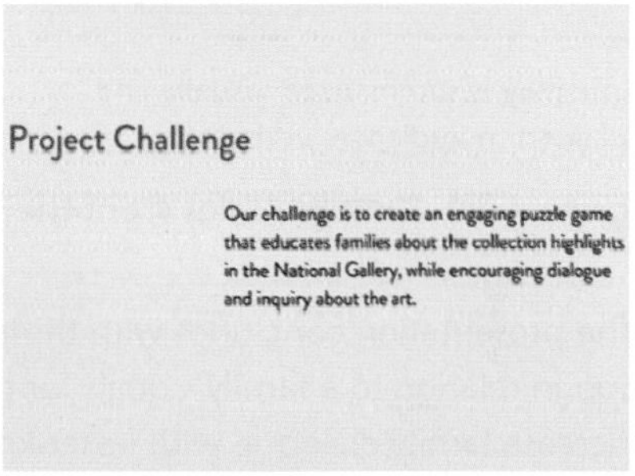

Figure 4.13 Project Purpose and Summary
Courtesy of Sarah Lowe

Next, the bulk of the presentation walked the audience through how the game would work for players—from the moment they walk into the museum exhibit to the conclusion of playing the app—a segment of the presentation that took thirty-nine slides. Sample slides walk audiences through the registration process, gameplay description, summary of the remaining four quests, and the conclusion screen (see **Fig. 4.14** on p. 106).

Individual players' registration screens.

Redd receives a gift—his pear—based on the artwork.

THANK YOU FOR HELPING ME OUT!

I wouldn't have been ready for the perfomance if it weren't for you! I had a great time, and we made some nice memories.

Game play is summarized visually and explained to audiences verbally.

Redd has received all his performance gifts.

Figure 4.14 Sample Slides from the Tales Pitch
Courtesy of Sarah Lowe

The presentation concludes with three slides reaffirming the value of this app in relation to a family's goals for playing and the museum's goals to increase family dialogue with lesser-known works of art. This summary in a pitch or proposal helps remind stakeholders that it's not just a cool game but also a learning tool that meets the objectives and outcomes they had desired. The team even went one step further in their verbal statement of values by suggesting that Redd the fox could be used as a branding tool, not just for this exhibit and app, but for the museum as a whole, thus providing a larger potential impact for the clients than originally anticipated (which clients usually appreciate).

The Feedback Loop

One of the reasons we wanted to use Tales as an extended case study for this book is because the project team did an excellent job pitching to stakeholders. In the feedback loop, there was very little critical feedback requiring the team to change anything substantial in their design or their final presentation to the museum. In addition, stakeholders found the fox compelling and likable, and we (as authors of *Writer/Designer*) knew that the way the team had presented Redd and the Tales prototype would recreate well in a printed book. So, we wanted to offer you a collaborative, student-based example that could be achieved by writer/

Figure 4.15
Just because we love this dang little fox.
He's so cute!
Courtesy of Sarah Lowe

designers who don't specialize in graphic design. Sure, Redd is pretty fancy, and we can't draw that well ourselves, but as a model—and perhaps with a little help from other collaborators who will make your work stronger—you can work towards this type of pitch and project.

write/design! assignment

Proposing to Get It All Done

This chapter's Case Study offered an inside look at a type of proposal called a design brief. Like most proposals, this one was used to document a project plan and to make a case for the strength and relevance of what the writer/designers intended to do. Proposals offer the opportunity to get feedback and to gain approval for moving forward with a project. Putting together your proposal will also be helpful as you design and build your project; it's a chance to make sure that you have a solid plan, that you have all the materials you'll need, that you know how to use the tools you want to use (or have a good plan for learning how to use them), and that you have a realistic schedule for getting everything done. (Learn more about using materials, tools, and schedules in Part Two of this book.)

You can use or adapt the outline of the design brief presented in the Case Study above to help write your proposal. Or here are some additional section headings and content ideas that will help convince your stakeholders you are ready to embark on this project:

- **Abstract.** Give a brief overview of what your project is about, how you will approach it, and what genre you will use to fit the rhetorical situation.

- **Justification.** Discuss why your proposed design is appropriate and effective for making your argument. (Knowing your genre and its conventions will be helpful here; see Chapter 3, pp. 64–67.) This justification might also include analyses you have completed of similar genres and texts for this audience. (As shown in the design brief Case Study, this section is sometimes called a "literature review" or "competitive analysis.")
- **Project description.** Fully describe your project concept and explain in detail what the rhetorical situation, genre, and audience will be. How will you design the project (including specific design elements, if known) to support your argument? Why do you need to use certain media, modes, or technologies to create a project that is useful to your particular audience? (See Chapter 7, Working with Technologies, for more on using different types of media and technology for your drafts and final texts.)
- **Roles and responsibilities.** If you're working with a group, identify which group members are responsible for which project activities. If you have a group contract, consider attaching it to the proposal. (See Chapter 5, Designing with Your Collaborators, on pp. 111–17 for more info on working collaboratively.)
- **Timeline.** Give a detailed work plan of how and when you will complete all the project's components. (See the Write/Design! option assignment at the end of this chapter for more details on creating project timelines.) Make sure to include a breakdown of your tasks at each stage:
  - doing further research
  - collecting, editing, and documenting assets
  - preparing a draft
  - getting feedback on your final draft
  - revising
  - delivering your project

write/design! option: Project Timeline

You can create timelines for any project, from an essay to an app design. Working backwards from your project's final due date, figure out how long each stage of development will take and make a plan. Be sure to build in time for getting feedback and revising. Collecting assets, building a prototype, and making changes to content in multimodal projects often takes longer than an author has planned for, whether it is because equipment becomes unavailable or because deadlines for other projects and meetings interrupt the author's work. It's not unusual to have to repeatedly revisit a project timeline to make adjustments for different obstacles and constraints, but creating a timeline now can help avoid a crisis later.

As you work out your timeline, consider the following issues:

- **Stages:** What are the major milestones you need to accomplish and in what order?
- **Logistics:** Are there any logistics you need to keep in mind as you proceed, such as computer lab hours, instructional technology checkout limits, spring break, other class commitments, travel, or the like?
- **Collaborators and responsibilities:** Since multimodal projects often require collaboration, it's important to establish who will be responsible for completing what and by when.
- **Contingency plans:** What will happen if your process gets off schedule? Have you built in any flex time? How will you adjust?

Although you can make a simple table in word processing or spreadsheet software to map out your timeline (like the one shown in **Fig. 4.16**), there are also a number of free online tools to create timelines visually. A Gantt chart (**Fig. 4.17** on p. 110) is a horizontal bar chart that illustrates the length of time key stages of a project will take, who will be responsible, and how those deadlines align with other activties in the development process.

Task	Project Dates					
	4/11	4/18	4/21	4/25	4/28	5/2
Discuss preliminary topic	All	All				
Complete proposal		A B C				
Complete timeline		B				
Begin research		All				
Complete research memo		C				
Team meeting with professor			All			
Ongoing research		All	All	All		
Draft report			A	A		
Edit and embedded images					B	
Workshop draft					A	
Revise report						C
Prepare presentation						B
Final revision and editing of report						All
Submit report						All
Deliver final presentation						All

A = Alice   B = Brett   C = Carol

Figure 4.16 A Simple Word Timeline

Courtesy of Jennifer Sheppard

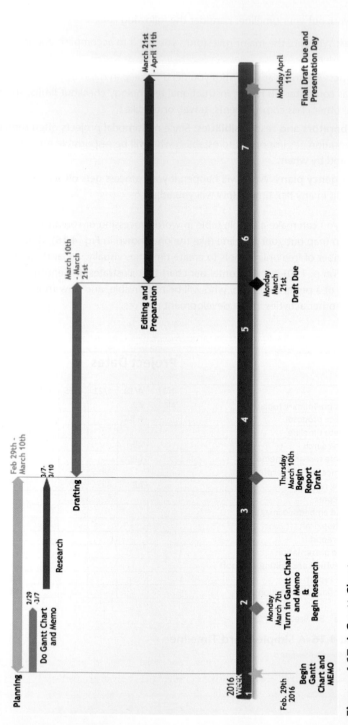

Figure 4.17 A Gantt Chart

Courtesy of Cody Archer, Cory Moore, Paul Jensen

How Do You Design and Revise with Multiple Audiences?

In Chapter 2, we discussed the various audiences that mutimodal projects can have, including primary audiences, such as readers and users, as well as secondary audiences, such as clients, stakeholders, teachers, colleagues, funding agencies, and others. Then, in Chapter 4, we showed you how one project team built the Tales app by considering their multiple audiences and getting feedback from some of them during the drafting process. This chapter takes you deep into that collaborative drafting process and the feedback loop with primary and secondary audiences of your own multimodal project. We start with collaborators because they are your project team and closest to you, but we also discuss what it's like to work on a multimodal project by yourself, which your project may call for. The second half of the chapter offers techniques for critiquing your multimodal work during the design process and creating a revision and delivery plan for your project.

Designing with Your Collaborators

Every reader of this book has likely had some kind of experience working with a group, and it's equally likely that not every collaborative experience has been a good one. As teachers and writer/designers, the three of us have certainly seen our fair share of collaborative projects go awry, whether because of conflict over the topic or direction of a project, personal disagreements among members of a group, or group members who don't contribute what they're supposed to. We also know firsthand, from the experience of writing this book together, that collaborating is hard work, especially when you have people who can't meet together in the same place and who have strong opinions on the way things should be done. However, this book wouldn't have been the same if any one of us had written it alone.

Collaborating with others, especially on multimodal projects, does have big benefits, but it can present complications that are better worked through from the beginning of a project. For instance, in the first edition of this textbook, we tried to use Google Drive to

Figure 5.1 Sharing Files with Dropbox

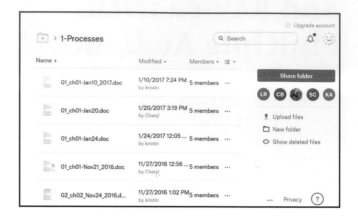

manage our authoring process and then migrated to Dropbox so that we could provide version control. For this version, we decided to use Dropbox from the very beginning (see **Fig. 5.1**). Because we had difficulty keeping track of versions in our first edition, the shared files followed a standard naming convention we'd created and were shared only among the three authors. (See Chapter 6, pp. 170–71 and 169–70 for more on version control and naming conventions.) In a separate folder, we shared final drafts with our editor, so she didn't have to get bogged down with our day-to-day progress. Sometimes we would all run into file-sharing problems, and miscommunications would lead to confusion. It happens even with the best of teams! So we start by providing strategies for keeping collaboration working and communication open among your teammates.

Strategies for Successful Collaboration

Just as every multimodal project is different, so is every collaborative situation, but there are some common strategies you can follow to make your group experience more successful and productive.

- If you have the option, limit the size of your team to between three and five members. Larger teams tend to have trouble coordinating schedules and coming to decisions (particularly when projects are designed as part of a class).

- If you get to choose your own team members, try to find others who will bring a diverse set of skills and perspectives to the process. Don't automatically choose friends or colleagues you already agree with. True collaboration means having divergent ideas and building consensus.

- Exchange contact information with the other team members, and commit to responding to them in a timely manner.

- Choose a preferred communication method where everyone on the team has access to the information they need at any time. Email and texting is often too difficult to keep track of. We recommend an online project management or communication tool—there are many freely available programs that support team-based work online. (See **Fig. 5.2.**)

- Create a group or team contract to spell out member expectations, such as roles, communication procedures, meeting guidelines, and problem-solving tactics.

- Be a good contributor—come to team meetings with all of your materials and with ideas about how to move the project forward. Just showing up and waiting around for someone to tell you what to do isn't really participation. And pull your own weight; nobody appreciates group members who don't complete their work.

- Be a good listener—collaborating requires that you listen to others' ideas. You don't always have to agree, but try to give people a chance to make their case.

- Remember that the most successful teams are often the ones whose members are flexible and are not so wedded to their

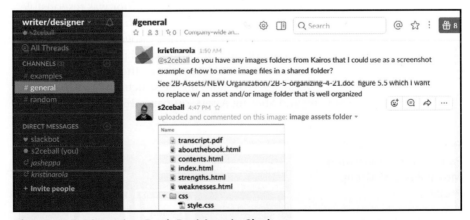

Figure 5.2 Discussing Book Revisions in Slack

The authors used Slack, a free communication tool that allows group chats and private messaging along with file uploads and linking to external services like Dropbox and Google Drive.

Cheryl Ball and Kristin Arola

ideas that they can't compromise. Being able to build off parts of one another's ideas can lead to some innovative and interesting possibilities.

- If your group faces *minor* conflict, try having a team meeting where members are asked to briefly share their perspectives on what's happening and their suggestions for resolving the issue.

- If your group faces *serious* conflict, talk to your instructor or supervisor, who will likely have strategies for helping to mediate and move forward.

Collaborative Workflow Options

One of the biggest challenges of group work on multimodal projects is finding a way to meaningfully involve all group members and to divide work fairly and reasonably. The following examples demonstrate how three student groups managed this challenge.

- **Divide the Work by Project Sections.** In one of Cheryl's classes, a student group created a webtext (a scholarly essay presented in multimedia form) about the visual rhetoric of movie posters in certain genres and across historical periods. The group decided that the project would have four main sections based on four movie genres and their representative posters: comedies, romantic comedies, action/thriller movies, and remakes (see **Fig. 5.3**). The four-person group divided the workload by movie genre so that each author was responsible for collecting assets and designing the Web page for a particular genre. The group members worked together to create the project's introduction and the works cited page. In **Figure 5.4**, the group's working file structure shows the breakdown of the project's workload. (For more on file structures, see Chapter 6, Organizing and Sharing Assets, on pages 166–171.)

Figure 5.3 Planned Home Page of the "Translating Movie Posters" Group Project

Courtesy of Casey Kilroy, Erin Lentz, Jess Krist, and Brian Sorenson

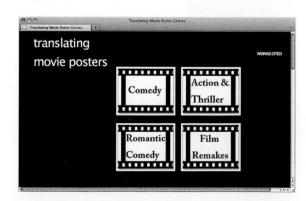

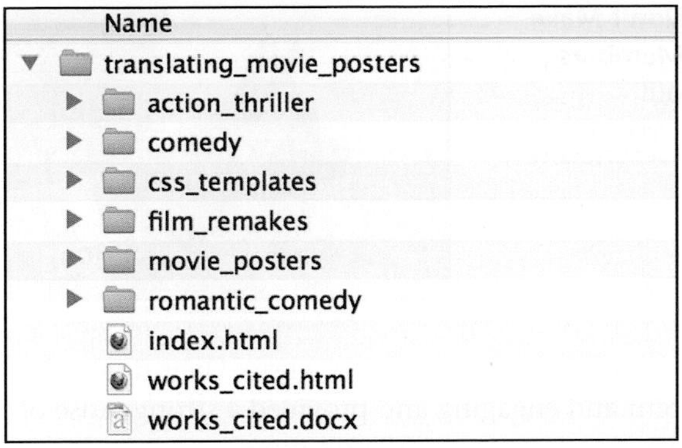

Name
▼ 📁 translating_movie_posters
▶ 📁 action_thriller
▶ 📁 comedy
▶ 📁 css_templates
▶ 📁 film_remakes
▶ 📁 movie_posters
▶ 📁 romantic_comedy
index.html
works_cited.html
works_cited.docx

Figure 5.4 File Structure of the "Translating Movie Posters" Project

Courtesy of Kristin Arola

- **Organize by Media Types and Expertise.** Another of Cheryl's student groups also created a webtext, this one about fashion and identity. The webtext included original fashion photos, video interviews of the authors discussing how fashion *shows* their identity, and scholarly sources that supported the visual components of the webtext. The three group members chose to break down their drafting process according to each student's expertise. Darien, an art and design major, was responsible for the website construction; Jenna, a publishing major, was responsible for the written text; and Bridget, a technical writing major, was responsible for the video editing. Because each member played to his or her strength, this small group was able to compose a large, ambitious project in a relatively short amount of time.

- **Organize by Compromise and Consensus.** The final student group, from Jenny's class, created an audio documentary on what it's like to be a search and rescue (SAR) team volunteer. The group was able to gather six hours of audio interviews, but then a critical issue emerged: How would the group decide which topics to develop and which to leave out due to time constraints? Each group member approached the project from a different perspective: one of them wanted to establish an "intellectually artful" feel, one wanted "to make an emotional appeal," and one wanted "to create a coherent story."

  Each member listened to all six hours of audio and took notes on the themes and compelling stories he or she thought should be included. The group members were committed to compromise and worked together to decide on a few basic themes for the documentary. In the end, all the members felt that they had been listened to and that their priorities had been accommodated. They all reported that the experience was frustrating at times but that their project was ultimately

Figure 5.5 Don't Make Your Group Members Search For You!

Bob Haarmans/Flickr, https://www.flickr.com/photos/rhaarmans/7279652198

stronger because of the combination of ideas. Their final project was coherent and engaging and provided a strong sense of the joys and stresses of being a SAR volunteer.

- **Write a Team Contract.** You and your fellow group members should start by discussing your group expectations. Use the lists in **Figure 5.6** to compose a team contract that spells out member expectations. Depending on your group project's rhetorical situation, you may decide to add other areas of concern to the contract. This contract will help hold your group accountable.

TEAM CONTRACT

Group Expectations

- What are our group goals for this project?
- What quality of work do we expect from each group member, and what strategies will we employ to fulfill these standards?
- How will we encourage ideas from all team members?

Tasks and Deadlines

- What tasks need to be completed by when, and by whom? What kinds of deadlines or milestones will we build into our write/design process?

Group Procedures

- What will be the dates, times, and locations of meetings?
- What is the preferred method of communication (online communication app, email, a project-management system, texting, phone calls, face-to-face meetings) for sharing information about meetings, updates, reminders, and problems?
- Where will assets and drafts be stored so that everyone who needs access has it?

Personal Accountability

- What strengths do individuals have that might make them more suited to one of the elements that needs to be produced more than others? How will you break up the workload?

- What is each team member's expected level of responsibility for attending meetings, responding to communication from other group members, and completing assigned tasks on time?

- How will the group handle a team member who does not comply with the contract? What are the consequences?

Signed,
Team Members

Figure 5.6 Questions for a Team Contract

⊙— Touchpoint: Planning with a Team

Imagine that your residence hall floor or a campus club you belong to has decided to enter this year's EarthWeek competition at your school. EarthWeek is a series of events that encourage, celebrate, and advocate for sustainability, campus spirit, and diversity.

EarthWeek requires each team to submit the following four elements to be eligible to participate in the campuswide competition:

1. A social media advertisement to inform the broader campus community about the EarthWeek event.

2. A one- to two-minute video advocating for the three pillars of EarthWeek: sustainability, diversity, and campus spirit.

3. An environmentally oriented game to teach visiting elementary students about sustainability and diversity at this year's festival.

4. An event of your own design that advocates and educates about at least one of the three pillars (you could arrange a special hike with a ranger at a nearby nature preserve, develop a composting program with campus restaurants and cafeterias, organize a beach cleanup, and lots more).

Given these requirements and this rhetorical situation, how would your team go about completing this work? Who will organize your first meeting to discuss initial ideas and how will it be run to maximize input and participation? What other issues do you need to address to make sure your team's entry is competitive? To help you plan, consider the questions in the Team Contract in **Figure 5.6**.

orking Alone

You can create a strong multimodal project on your own, but there are a few useful things to remember.

- Working alone because you hate working in groups undercuts the potential of any project you might create. With others, you have more ideas, skills, and talents to work with.

- Since you won't have team members to bounce ideas off of, be sure to do a thorough job in preparing your pitch presentation and proposal (see Chapter 4). Doing so will allow you to get critical feedback from your instructor, classmates, or other stakeholders so that you can make adjustments as needed.

- Keep the size of your project manageable. Since you will be doing all the research, asset gathering, composing, and editing, you'll want to focus the scope of your ideas.

- Since you'll be solely responsible for the composing, seek out support for any technologies with which you're unfamiliar. We want to encourage you to try new genres, but if you run into trouble or have questions, consult with local resources, online tutorials, or friends. Just because you're working alone doesn't mean you can't get feedback or assistance from others.

◉— Touchpoint: **Working Alone Isn't Really Working Alone**

If it's not obvious from the tips above, we don't really believe it's possible to work absolutely by yourself on a project. There is always someone (or something) to provide feedback, advice, or information. In our own professional lives, we have found a mentoring map to be surprisingly helpful to identify who might provide support—and a feedback loop—on a large project.

Think about the network of people who will support you and give you feedback on the work for which you're using this book. Then, fill out the map below. Keep it with you throughout your projects, adding people or groups as you discover them.

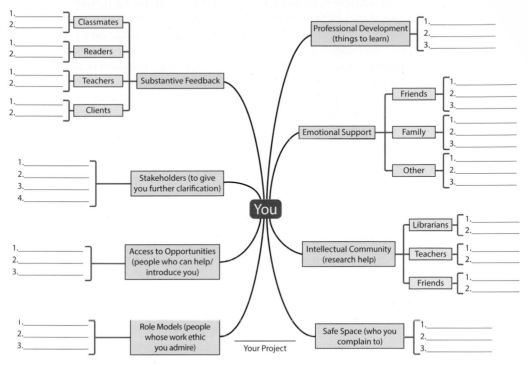

Figure 5.7 Mentoring Map

This map is adapted from the National Center for Faculty Development and Diversity mentoring map (www.facultydiversity.org). Fill in the lines or draw your own to map your support network.

With permission of National Center for Faculty Development and Diversity

Finalizing Drafts for Your Primary Audience

While team members and your support network function as one type of audience you work with when you're building your multi modal project, your primary audience for the project and its needs are always the most important. Because *how* the project progresses will also be dependent on what media and technologies you're working in, we have reserved discussion of those possibilities for Chapter 7, where you can pick and choose which you plan to make (i.e., analog or digital, dynamic or static, etc.). You might be drafting an outline, mock-up, storyboard, or prototype, depend- ing on the media and technology choices that are appropriate to r audience. In any case, your project will move through various stages of "roughness," from a collection of ideas and media assets to a more polished draft. In later drafts, all the assets should be finely edited and in place so that the project will work without any intervention by the author. That is, while your roughest drafts don't have to work—they are prototypes of what you *hope* will work—your polished draft should be usable by your primary audience in the technology and the medium that you will eventually distribute your project in.

A Checklist for Final Drafts

Use the following list as a starting point of things to check for as you prepare the polished draft of your project for audience feedback.

❑ All written content has been finalized, edited, and proofread.

❑ All visual and aural elements (photos, illustrations, logos, videos, audio clips) have been edited in the appropriate software to their exact lengths or sizes and converted to the correct formats and resolutions, and they have been placed in their exact locations within the project.

❑ Fonts, text sizes, and color schemes have been implemented consistently throughout the document.

❑ Styles (when appropriate) have been used, and style guides have been followed.

❑ Animations (title screens, visual transitions, object movement) have been edited, synced for appropriate duration on screen, and placed in their final locations in the project.

❑ Color photocopies of all visual elements have been printed at the quality needed.

❑ Soundtracks or other whole-project media elements have been edited for appropriate volume, added to the timeline, and synced to the individual scenes or navigation.

❑ Navigation or movement within the project (prezi path, slideshow autoplay, Web menu, performance blocking) has been created and finalized.

❑ Nothing is broken (images are in place, links work, videos don't stall, programs don't crash).

❑ The analog project is available in its final medium (printed poster, folded brochure) or the digital project has been exported from its editing program (Word, InDesign, Publisher, Movie Maker, iMovie, Audacity, Dreamweaver, KompoZer) into the final output format (converted to a PDF, MOV, or MP3 file; moved onto a Web server).

You might consult your instructor, boss, other stakeholders, and/or intended audience at any stage, but once you have a completed draft (following the guidelines above), you should definitely seek feedback, even though it may not be totally ready for public release.

Delivering Drafts for Peer Review

How do you know whether your project works and whether it's ready for an initial review by your stakeholders? Start by testing it yourself to see how easily an audience will be able to navigate and make sense of your text. You can gather useful information on how functional your project is and fix errors before the project goes to your audience. This is like proofreading an essay: the paper draft is done and you think it's ready to be turned in, but you know your teacher will catch some places where you are missing transitions or have misspellings; so you print out the paper and read it through to try to catch those issues before turning it in. Preparing and testing the rough draft of your multimodal project has the same purpose. How you prepare will depend on which media and technologies you're using.

A useful review provides feedback on an author's in-progress (but hopefully nearly completed) work. When stakeholders provide feedback, they often intuitively understand the rhetorical situation and genre expectations of a text. Sometimes, however, reviewers don't know how to evaluate a project because they are not familiar with the particular situation or genre or because they are used to working on other kinds of projects.

For instance, in the following example, a group of English department faculty members at West Virginia University, each with varying design expertise (from none to significant), discussed changes to a rough draft of an affirmation poster. The poster was designed in response to the rise in hate speech after the 2016 elections and a presidential Executive Order in early 2017 enacting a travel ban from Muslim countries. The English department wanted to hang the poster in the foyer to its campus building (see **Fig. 5.8**) as a way to encourage community building and unity through compassion and ethical communication. Because the English department faculty had expertise in language, the wording of the statement was completed quickly, through multiple rounds of feedback. But inserting the statement into a designed poster presented some feedback challenges. The poster, designed quickly by a local copy shop, was first distributed as an 8.5 x 11-inch color printout in a department meeting. That version was easy to pass around for comments, especially since the final poster was meant to be a large-scale 3 x 6-foot vertical poster, which would have been impossible to pass around to the thirty stakeholders present. Reviewers made various points about the colors, typeface, and styles used in the poster. The more experienced design faculty noted that the design didn't quite meet the accepted WVU branding schema. After that initial review of the rough draft and several design revisions in Adobe InDesign by faculty members, a PDF was distributed on the department listserv and the final poster was approved and printed.

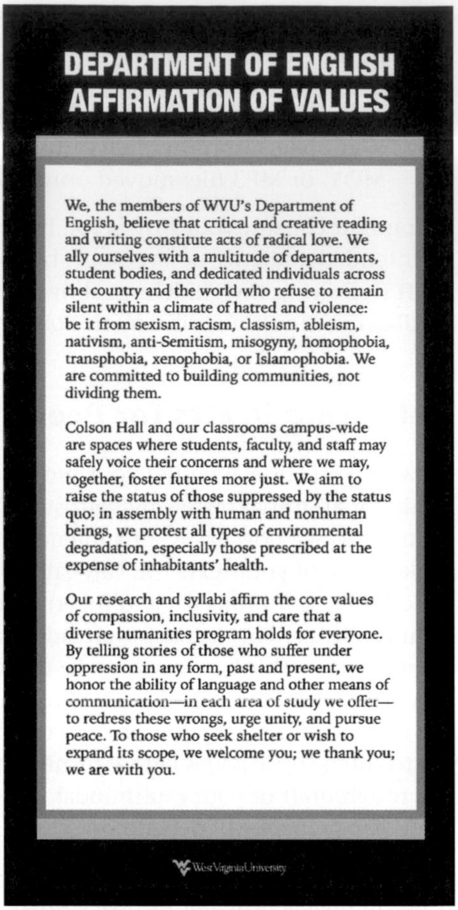

Figure 5.8 Final Draft of WVU Affirmation Poster

Courtesy of West Virginia University Department of English

This is a brief example about how the formats of projects and stakeholders' knowledge of the project constraints might help (or sometimes hinder) getting feedback on your project. We discuss peer review more in the second half of this chapter, but there are other documents you can provide stakeholders to help them understand how to review your project. We detail these in the next section.

Touchpoint: Preparing Audiences for Feedback with a Delivery Plan

As you prepare to deliver your project for review, consider the questions that follow. If your project is not yet ready for this stage, use this activity to plan for the review process for a future project, such as a research paper or advertisement for your next performance, game, or other event.

Understanding a project's rhetorical situation will prepare audiences to better provide feedback for projects, so prepare a delivery plan that summarizes your project's situation by addressing some of the following questions:

- Who is the **intended audience** for this piece, and what rhetorical moves do you make to appeal to these readers/listeners/viewers/users?

- How well is the **purpose** of the project conveyed through its organization/navigation? Is there a coherent message for the audience to follow? Do you offer commentary (the "so what" of the argument or story)?

- How do the **design choices** (emphasis, contrast, organization, alignment, and proximity) help enact your purpose?

- Do the **mode**, **media**, and **genre** choices contribute to the overall purpose and meaning conveyed by the project?

As an author, you should also be able to accommodate your readers' interaction with your delivery method as you prepare for them to give you feedback. Will they view your text onscreen? If so, what kind of screen will they view it on—desktop, laptop, mobile, tablet? Where will they view it? In the library, in their home office, in a classroom, on a train? Will they view it over a wireless or an Ethernet connection?

- Where does the review take place?

- As the author, am I expected to be present during the review?

- If so, what are the presentation expectations? Is it formal or informal? What is the expected attire?

- If not, how will I provide reviewers with my draft?

- What technologies are available for them to review my project? For me to review their project?

- What's the timeline for reviewing? Will the review of each other's work take place at the same time? Do we each have a few days to review the work? What's the deadline?

- In what medium are the reviews to be conducted? If multimedia reviews are acceptable, is the author able to view reviews that are made in proprietary programs?

Peer Reviewing Multimodal Projects

While you may be eager to hear commentary about your own project, providing feedback to your colleagues can be equally valuable in terms of helping you think about different and successful approaches to multimodal projects. As a reviewer of someone else's work, you have three main tasks:

1. **Read the text** from the perspective of a particular audience member or rhetorical situation for which that text is intended (the summary of rhetorical situation and genre conventions is intended to assist readers with understanding this perspective).

2. **Evaluate** whether the text is successful at meeting the criteria and expectations required by that rhetorical situation.

3. **Provide constructive feedback** to the author based on the text's effectiveness (or ineffectiveness).

Read the Text

When reviewing a text, you should begin by familiarizing yourself with the rhetorical situation and genre expectations of the project. A summary or checklist like the one we recommended you create for the Touchpoint exercise, Preparing Audiences for Feedback with

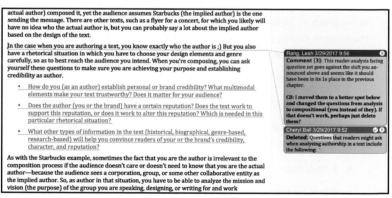

Figure 5.9 A Rough Draft in Microsoft Word

We had plenty of rough drafts for the first edition of this book—more than twenty, in fact—and another half-dozen for the second edition. Each time that we made revisions (using our editor and each other as our feedback loop), we used the Track Changes feature in Word (as shown in this example). Once our editor approved the revisions, we cleared them out (by accepting them) and continued revising other sections that still needed work.

a Delivery Plan (p. 123), can be useful if you are unfamiliar with the genre, intended audience, or other elements of the rhetorical situation.

You may need time to figure out how the text works and why it works the way it does, and to discover whether there are elements of what the author has designed that you like (or don't like). Being an active reviewer—trying to figure out what the author's reasoning was for a particular design choice or rhetorical decision—will aid you in providing constructive feedback. In other words, don't just assume an author did it wrong. (Remember our lolcat from the opening chapter?) As you read, take notes on how and why you respond to the piece. This is where the summary of the rhetorical situation created by the author can serve as a touchstone for evaluating the project.

Evaluate the Text

Based on your reading of the project, it's your job as a reviewer to evaluate how effectively the designer hits the rhetorical mark. As a reader, do you feel that the project meets your needs and expectations? Does it miss anywhere? For each question or comment that you pose to the author, you should be able to include discussion of *why* and *how* in your review.

Here are some suggested questions to ask yourself as you evaluate the text:

- Does the project match the expected **rhetorical situation** and **genre conventions** to meet the audience's needs? If not, does it break those conventions in productive ways that serve the audience?

- How do the **mode**, **media**, and **genre** choices contribute to the overall purpose and meaning conveyed by the project? Are there any you would add or delete, and if so, why?

- Is the **design** of this project appropriate to its **purpose**? If some design choices seemed inappropriate in relation to the rhetorical situation, what suggestions would you make for revising?

- How credible do you find the **assets** and **sources** used for the project's argument? (See Chapter 6 for more information on these.) Were there any sources you found problematic? If so, which ones and why, and what would you suggest be used in their place? Were there sources missing that you'd suggest for the project?

Provide Constructive Feedback

In preparing your review from your reading notes, you should identify the main strengths and weaknesses of the project, summarizing your thoughts about how well the piece addresses the rhetorical situation. Discuss how the piece meets (or doesn't meet) the project criteria, and provide formal and constructive feedback, including revision suggestions whenever possible. In many cases, reviews of rough drafts are written up and provided to the authors so that they can refer to the review comments throughout the revision process. Those review comments provide overarching commentary on the status of the piece, summarizing what suggestions you have for further strengthening this author's approach or for better attending to the target audience. They can also offer specific revision suggestions.

Here are some tips for writing a useful review:

- Use the beginning of the review to summarize the project's purpose back to the author, which helps the author see whether you understood the piece in the way that he or she intended or in a different way.

- Be generous in your reading, and be helpful and productive in explaining what's not working in the piece and how you think the author should revise the project. Use a tone that will help the author take in your advice rather than just be offended by it. Help the author recognize what is working so that he or she can build on those positive aspects in revising.

- The review should usually address revision suggestions in a hierarchical way, moving from the biggest issues to the smallest issues. Small issues are sometimes left out of the review if big picture issues overwhelm the project. For example, it may not be important that a project has some grammatical errors if it's not hitting the mark as far as its overall purpose.

- Alternately, a review might be structured as a reader response—that is, it might follow the reader's chronological progression through the text. But summaries at the beginning and end of the review are still helpful in contextualizing the reviewer's minute-by-minute commentary.

- Always explain why and how a project is or isn't working well, and make sure that your revision suggestions are clear, even if your revision ideas are more like suggestions than must-dos.

⊙— Touchpoint: Giving Feedback on a Rough Draft

Ask your client, classmates, or instructor to review your multimodal project, and offer your services as a reviewer in turn. Using the questions outlined in the Peer Reviewing Multimodal Projects section above, write a peer-review letter to another author that follows the tips and steps for giving constructive feedback: (1) read the text, (2) evaluate the text, and (3) provide constructive feedback on the text.

You might also consider creating more specific peer-review questions for the genre of text you are reviewing. For instance, students in one of Jenny's classes used the following questions to peer review a genre-analysis infographic. How can you rephrase some of these to get at the reading, evaluation, and constructive feedback of your own peer-review letter?

- Who is the **audience** and how can you tell? Is there any information that needs to be added or taken away to make it more useful to target readers?

- What is the **purpose** of this project? That is, what do you take away as a reader and how well does this seem to match up with the intentions of the writer/designer?

- Has the designer followed the **KISS (keep it simple, stupid) principle**? Is there too much or too little information? If so, what suggestions do you have?

- What **design principles** are used and in what ways are they relevant to **emphasize** significant content (**contrast**), maintain visual unity (**repetition**), **organize** information, and group related content (**alignment, proximity, framing**)? What suggestions do you have for improvement?

- Name one thing that the **designer does particularly well** in this draft.

- What other suggestions or ideas do you have for improving the message of the text?

CASE STUDY

Revising an Advertisement Design with Stakeholder Feedback

As part of her job, Cheryl helps a nonprofit organization called the Council of Editors of Learned Journals (CELJ). This organization is composed of hundreds of scholarly journal editors who discuss editorial issues related to their individual journals in a private, online forum where they can seek advice and information from other editors in a confidential manner. One of the member benefits for journal editors is a discounted advertisement in an internationally renowned glossy magazine called the *Times Literary Supplement* (*TLS*), and the CELJ gets a free advertisement each year in the *TLS* because of all the additional ad revenue it brings to the *TLS* through its members. (All of this is **context** for the *what*, which comes next.) The *TLS* sent Cheryl the following email to forward to members, reminding them to place their ads, including CELJ's own ad.

Dear CELJ Member, ●──────────────────── **Stakeholder**

Context

The *Times Literary Supplement* is the world's oldest and most reputable literary journal. It is published every Friday, and reviews thousands of books every year. It has a growing circulation—currently around 28,000
Audience
per week—and its readers are mature, affluent, and well educated.

Purpose

Client
The October 28th issue of the *TLS* will offer members of the CELJ the opportunity to advertise their journals at half the regular price.

Additional context about visual layout, organization

This issue will carry three or four pages of reviews of journals, and another 3 or 4 pages of advertising.

Genre conventions
Advertising in this issue starts at £57.50 for the minimum 5cm x 6.3cm box, and there is a huge range of sizes available.

If you have any questions, or if you would like to book some space in this
Stakeholder
issue, please contact email-redacted@tlk.uk. The deadline for this issue is
Context (due date)
fast approaching—space needs to be confirmed before October 14th.

Cheryl knew the **audience** would be educated and well-read readers of the *Times Literary Supplement*, which is a premier print-based literary and cultural magazine that has been around for over 100 years. But the CELJ ad didn't need to target just *any* reader of the *TLS*; it needed to target editors of literary and scholarly journals who read the *TLS*. Cheryl had to design the ad to effectively target readers of *TLS* who were also editors, to persuade them to join CELJ.

Cheryl (as an intermediate stakeholder/client) asked Lydia, a project team member, to design a rough draft of the ad that Cheryl could modify or approve before sending it to the magazine for publication. This email helped Lydia understand the rhetorical situation for designing the ad. Cheryl instructed Lydia to use the following elements in her draft of the ad: the CELJ logo, a list of the organization's member benefits, a link to its website, and the sponsoring institution (their university library). Lydia was able to easily gather all those assets from other projects she had worked on with Cheryl to design a draft of the ad well before the deadline. (Chapter 6, Working with Multimodal Assets and Sources, in Part Two of this book offers tips on how to gather design assets, like Lydia did for the above advertisement.)

But not all of the context Lydia needed to design the ad was present in the initial email that the *TLS* sent out. For instance, she had to ask several questions of the contact person at the magazine:

1. What size/dimensions could CELJ use?

2. Where would the final advertisement appear—online or in print? (The delivery medium would impact color choices and the image resolution.)

3. If it would appear in print, what kind of paper did the magazine use? (Printing on matte, glossy, or newsprint paper requires different design techniques that affect how the ink soaks into the paper.)

4. If in print, would the ad appear in black-and-white or color (and if the latter, how many colors was she allowed—since color printing can often come in variants of one, two-, three-, or four-color combinations)?

5. Finally, in what technical format would they prefer delivery of the ad file(s)? (JPEG, PNG, etc.)

In this case, the ad would appear only in the printed version of the magazine, alongside other ads for journals. The magazine gave advertisers two options for sending: either a designed ad in the form of a 10-cm high x 13-cm wide PDF, or text and logos so the magazine could design the ad. Cheryl and Lydia decided to send a designed ad so they would have more control over the CELJ branding. The magazine did not give any color restrictions, but Cheryl and Lydia chose to design the ad minimalistically, with the single, blue color that matches the CELJ logo and website branding. They also knew that since the ad would appear alongside several other journal advertisements on a single page, they wanted the CELJ ad to stand out from the crowd and so used white space to accomplish that goal.

Lydia was nervous. She didn't think she was a good visual designer, so the task of designing an ad was daunting. But she stepped up to the challenge and designed several mock-ups and drafts, delivering them to Cheryl for initial feedback as both a Portable Document Format (PDF) and a Photoshop Data file (.psd) (see **Fig. 5.10**). Lydia knew that Cheryl had access to Adobe Photoshop, an image manipulation program installed on her computer, so it was OK to send her a copy of the editable .psd file. But if Cheryl hadn't had Photoshop, she would not have been able to open or view the .psd file. (That's why it's important to remember to send your reviewers project and file types they can open and read, just like you would in the final version of the text.)

Lydia worked diligently to manipulate Photoshop to produce an initial draft in **Figure 5.10**. Later that same day, when she was on a computer without Photoshop, she continued to create mock-ups of her ideas using PowerPoint (**Fig. 5.11**). It's typical for designers to create three to four mock-ups or roughly designed drafts for the client to choose from. (In this case, Cheryl would choose for CELJ.) Lydia's primary concern at this point was to make sure the layout of the ad met the constraints given by the magazine: the size and dimension requirements.

Cheryl liked the general direction Lydia was heading with the Photoshop draft. She provided feedback for Lydia to revise the ad so it made better

Council of Editors
of Learned Journals

MEMBER BENEFITS   JOIN TODAY

- Guaranteed exhibit space at MLA   For more information,
- Advertising discount at Times Literary   visit celj.org.
  Supplement
- Access to a members-only editorial discussion
  forum
- Outreach opportunities with editors
  nationwide

Figure 5.10 Initial Draft of the Ad in Photoshop
Courtesy of the Council of Editors of Learned Journals

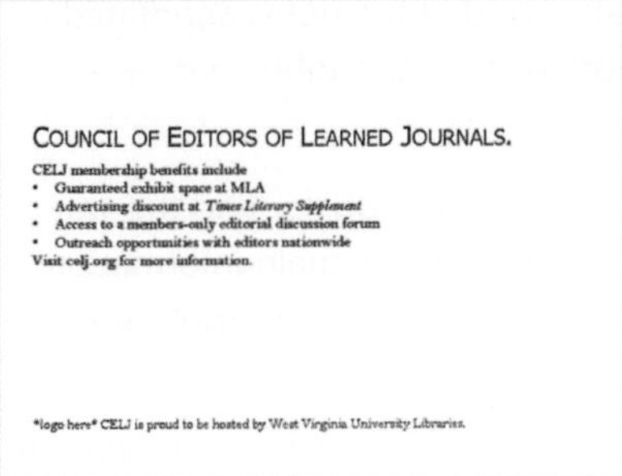

Mock-Up #1 Lydia played with variations of alignments and white space.

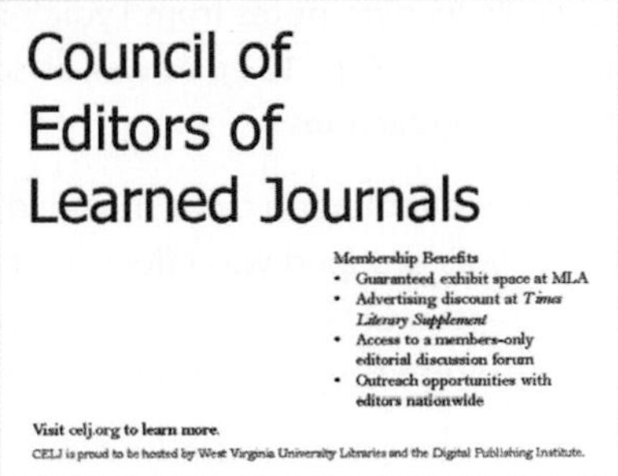

Mock-Up #2 Lydia played with minimal alignment and white space even more.

Figure 5.11 PowerPoint Mock-ups

Courtesy of the Council of Editors of Learned Journals

use of the **design concepts** Lydia had started with, including her attention to proximity, alignment, color, organization, and emphasis. Cheryl could have written up the feedback for Lydia but decided to meet with her instead to show her some additional design resources she could draw on to feel more comfortable designing such ads in the future.

The color of the CELJ "header" matches the logo for visual repetition and cohesion. But the thinness of the CELJ header font counteracts its level of emphasis, and there was a lot of space between the top and second rows of that header.

The dashes used as bullet points and the lack of hanging indents on the list made this rough draft seem rougher than it needed to be. The *TLS* would expect a little more polish.

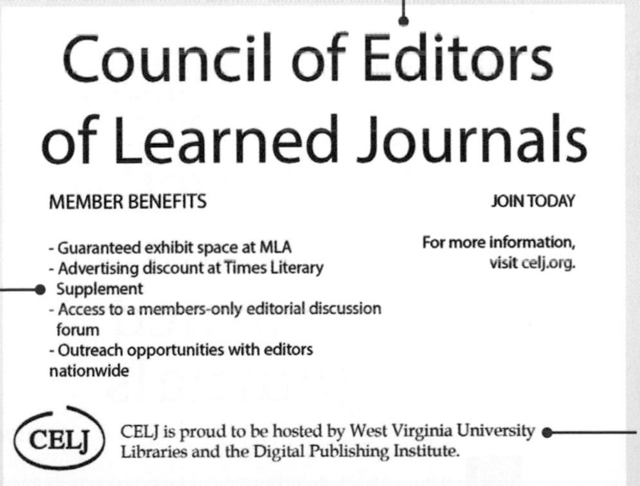

The footer information, with the logo, should be centered to retain alignment with the header and body copy, as well as to avoid trapped white space in the lower right corner.

Figure 5.12 Cheryl's Feedback on the Draft

Courtesy of Cheryl Ball

Cheryl's reading notes from Lydia's first draft included the notes annotated in **Figure 5.12** (p. 131), as well as some more general thoughts, perspectives, and reactions:

- The information Lydia included in the ad was appropriate, and the way it was grouped was effective. It's easy to tell what the main information is—the CELJ header, Member Benefits, and Join Today are emphasized through size, color, and all caps.

- The design was fuzzy for some reason (this could be OK for a rough draft, but not a final draft).

- The varying fonts—*serif* in the "footer" copy versus *sans serif* in the "body" copy—were easy to read on their own, but together they conflicted with each other in style and color.

- The left and right alignments were working well, with a two-column layout.

After revising based on Cheryl's feedback, Lydia and Cheryl produced the version shown in **Figure 5.13**. In this version, they changed the fonts so that the CELJ header font more closely matched the font used in the logo and made the header the central feature of the ad, with smaller spacing between each line, which gives the words better **proximity** to show their grouping as a single **linguistic** element in the ad. Lydia and Cheryl also removed the bullet points in the benefits listing so that its sentence-like structure would work with the footer copy to **frame** the CELJ header as

Figure 5.13
The Final Version of the CELJ Ad

Courtesy of the Council of Editors of Learned Journals

MEMBER BENEFITS
Members-only discussion forum, guaranteed exhibit space at MLA, discounted ads in *TLS*, outreach to new authors and editors

Council of Editors of Learned Journals

http://celj.org

 CELJ is proud to be hosted by West Virginia University Libraries' Digital Publishing Institute.

the ad's focal point. In addition, the footer was edited so it would all fit on one line, while still retaining its original meaning. The shorter line also added white space above the footer, further emphasizing the CELJ header. Finally, since the ad would appear amidst several pages with nothing but advertisements for other journals and on a white, printed background, they added one final touch: a thin, blue stroke, or outline, for **emphasis** and **contrast**.

Finally, the *TLS* requested a PDF of the ad output from Photoshop, which Cheryl and Lydia did by sending them a link to a filesharing location because—due to the print nature of the ad, which requires higher resolutions and larger file sizes than digitally distributed ads— the file was too large to send as an email attachment. It appeared several months later in the printed magazine alongside other ads (see **Fig. 5.14**).

Figure 5.14 The Final Version of the CELJ Ad in the Printed *TLS* (middle, left)

Courtesy of Karen Lunsford

Revising Your Multimodal Project

After you have received feedback on your rough draft from your peers, instructor, and/or stakeholders, it's time to evaluate the suggestions and make plans for revision. Try to consider *why* reviewers responded in the way that they did and whether there are changes you can make so that you get the kind of reaction you were intending. For instance, in the CELJ Case Study, the change of spacing, proximity, emphasis, and other design choices during revision helped the advertisement more clearly stand out for readers amid a sea of other ads.

Creating a Revision Plan

After reviewing all feedback, you should assess which revisions are important given your project goals, noting that sometimes reviewers have bad days, or they don't understand your rhetorical situation (because they aren't the intended audience). But don't let yourself be fooled into thinking that you are always right and that your project doesn't need any revisions. If a majority of your reviewers indicated that your font choice will give your audience the willies or that your script's tone is condescending, they are probably right. In addition, if a majority of your reviewers didn't mention a particular problem, but one reviewer made a *really good argument* for revising and backed it up with evidence from your text and your rhetorical situation summary, it's likely that the suggestion is a good one, and you'll need to consider addressing it as well.

Paying close attention to the feedback you've received, create a revision plan for your project. Here are some questions to help you determine which revisions you need to make:

- What were the strengths of my draft that I should be sure to keep?

- What design choices were problematic, and how can I revise these?

- What rhetorical choices seemed out of place in my draft, and how can I better attend to my audience, purpose, context, and genre?

- What multimodal elements can I add or revise to strengthen the rhetorical effect and credibility of my project?

- What are the most important changes I need to consider as I revise?

- Given the time and technology constraints of this project, what can I reasonably revise before the next due date? What else would need revision that I don't have time to complete but *should* complete, given enough time and resources?

That last question in the list is an important one. Most projects have a set deadline, whether it's a class project, a client's product-reveal date, or an event on the calendar. You and your reviewers may agree during the feedback loop and discussion of the revision plan that your original scope of work outlined in a proposal or assignment is too large to complete by the deadline but that a modified version of the project would be suitable for now. As long as you both agree to the modifications, it is fine to scale back on the scope of your project. In fact, scaling back may even strengthen your project.

Finalizing Your Project

After you've agreed to a revision plan, revise your rough draft into your final project. Your task is to make recommended changes and put the finishing touches on your project so that it accomplishes all your rhetorical goals. You will want to ensure that

- all of the multimodal elements you've included are purposeful;
- all of the multimodal elements support the credibility of your project;
- your audience can understand and navigate or read your text as you intend.

Test your project by using it in a venue as close to its final publication or presentation location as possible. For instance, if you're making a video for a nonprofit organization that is meant to be shared through social media, try uploading the video to the location you will share it from—but only if you can mark the video as Private so that it won't be released to the public before it's ready. Then share the private URL with a few key stakeholders or peers to see whether they think the revisions you've done match your rhetorical intentions. They may not have seen the original draft, so you might ask them key questions targeted to the purpose of the revisions after they've viewed it. That way, you won't end up with unnecessary revisions that this new audience prefers but that are not in the wishes of the client. Tweak the project based on their feedback, revising as necessary until you're satisfied that the text does its rhetorical work or until you're out of time.

Touchpoint: Revising Your Project

Using the suggested questions in the Creating a Revision Plan section (pp. 134–35), design a revision plan for your project that you can use as a task list for yourself or as a part of the documentation you hand over to stakeholders (discussed in the next section, Creating Documentation for Your Stakeholders) if you don't have time to complete the revisions yourself. There are dozens of to-do apps online. Find one that suits your team's needs and use it to create a sharable revision plan with assigned tasks. Alternatively, create a shared list in Google Drive or a content management system that team members and stakeholders, such as your instructor, can view and use.

Creating Documentation for Your Stakeholders

While your primary audience takes priority in your design process, your prioritizations in a project are almost always built on other stakeholder's expectations, such as grading criteria developed by a teacher, project specs provided by a client, the budget available from a funding agency, and so on. When you work with stakeholders, keep their needs and expectations in mind throughout and even after the design process, since many times you might need to turn the project over to them upon its completion—either so they can archive it, continue running it, or update it in the future, as needed.

Clients will often continue working on projects after you've finished designing them, especially if you're volunteering, getting paid with one-time grant funds, or participating in a service-learning class. Projects such as newsletters, training materials, blogs, and other serialized or continually updated texts often have a series of people working on them, which increases the likelihood that the texts will remain active and useful. **Documentation** explains how a project was created, how to use it, or how to update it in the future. Writing documentation can also help project teams collaborate while they are drafting and serve as accessibility documentation for primary or secondary readers with different abilities who may not be able to read all of the media and modes you plan to use.

There are many kinds of documentation, such as white papers, reference manuals, online help files, and user guides. We explain two types of documentation methods: wikis and comments. Depending on your project, you may need one or both of those methods, or you may use some other method or combination of methods to convey your processes to your client. No matter which documentation method you choose, the rhetorical considerations we've used throughout this book will be effective when considering medium, genre, or technology.

Collaborative Wiki

In **Figure 5.15**, you can see some of the documentation developed by a team of student writer/designers who created an online literary arts magazine called *Din*. The students who created *Din* wanted future classes of students to be able to put out new editions of the magazine. They decided to use a wiki for their documentation, which allows all registered users to add to and edit the text. This wiki contains specifics about what design elements (in relation to rhetorical choices) the design group used to distribute iterations of the magazine to social media, on a blog, and on Facebook; it also hosts an archive of promotional materials and logo designs. In the future, the documentation wiki could easily be changed as needed. To see how editors comment on their changes to wikis, go to *Wikipedia*, search for a term related to your project, and click that entry's "View history" tab to see what kind of changes have happened recently.

Figure 5.15 Project Documentation in a Wiki

The project documentation for *Din* illustrates and discusses logo and visual design choices (http://dinguidebook.wikispaces.com).

Courtesy of Jen Almjeld

In-Line Comments

A website designer will often embed comments into the HTML code to help future designers understand the designer's thought process when creating the site. Comments do not show up on the actual Web page but are viewable in the source code and in Web-editing programs like Dreamweaver or KompoZer. In the comment shown in **Figure 5.16**, the designer of this webtext—an author known by readers of his text as an expert in HTML—provides context for his non-standard usage of HTML coding and instructions on how to engage with it if someone is using a screen reader. If you are working on a project that is not Web-based, you could use the marginal comments and balloons in word-processing programs to achieve a similar purpose.

To see this source code documentation at work, go to a website that you use often and view its code. (The code is sometimes found under View > Source, or you can search for instructions for finding the source code if it's not readily apparent.) How did the designers of the site use HTML commenting? If they didn't use commenting, are there places where it would have been useful?

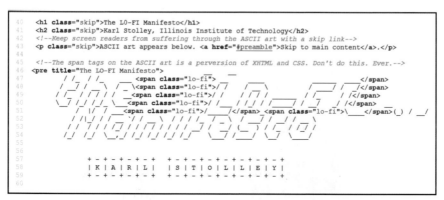

Figure 5.16 Source Code Comments Can Provide Help for Future Users
Courtesy of Karl Stolley

⊚— Touchpoint: **Creating a Style Guide**

Documentation comes in many forms, including style guides. A style guide is a set of agreed-upon standards that a group uses to write, design, and edit documents. For example, look at the branding page for West Virginia University (http://brand.wvu.edu/). Brands include style guides, and this website outlines why the "Mountaineers Go First!" rallying cry isn't just

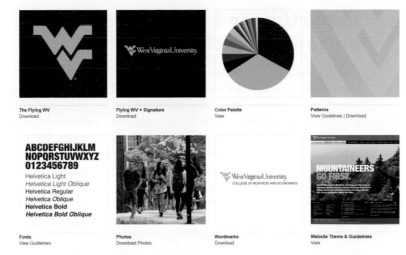

Figure 5.17 A Snapshot of the WVU Brand Center's Style Guide for Multiple Genres, Modes, and Text Usages

West Virginia University

for football games: "Having the courage to go first doesn't mean going impulsively without a plan. Going first is about making bold, but informed decisions. As writers, designers, photographers, web developers and overall brand ambassadors, all of us are called upon to go forth and help shape our brand. This guide will direct you—ensuring that we communicate consistently and powerfully." Take a look at this style guide online to find out what branding options the WVU English Department used for its affirmation poster, seen in **Figure 5.8** (p. 122).

Now, create your own style guide for your multimodal project using the guidelines here. (You may need to refer to the appropriate sections in Part Two of this book to answer some of these questions. It's OK to skip ahead and read those now, then return to this Touchpoint later.)

1. Discuss with your project team the best way to organize, share, and design your assets, based on the best practices you have found through your research and drafting.

2. Include plans for naming, storing, and sharing assets and style instructions.

3. Include a brief description of why your group has chosen to follow this particular style, based on the technologies you plan to use and the kinds of assets you found.

4. Decide where you will maintain your project style guide and how team members and stakeholders will have access to refer to and update it, as needed.

Reporting and Reflecting on Your Project

You may be asked to provide **reports** throughout the multimodal composition process for your instructor or stakeholders. Interim reports are usually written summaries of key progress made on the project, although they might occasionally be oral presentations. End-of-project reporting can be many different genres, including presentations, written reports, white papers, technical papers, scholarly articles, news features, and less formal genres such as blog posts, reflections, and exit interviews. In any of these genres, you have an opportunity to demonstrate to your audience the value of what you've done and (in some cases) the reasoning that got you to that point. If you are required to report on your multimodal project, keep in mind that your task is to be persuasive, not just descriptive. Help your audience understand each of the major design and rhetorical choices you've made and how those choices were appropriate to that particular rhetorical situation. **Reflecting** on your research and design processes as well as on your final project also allows you to see just how much you've learned and how you might approach your next project differently to make it even stronger and more efficient.

Sometimes reports indicate when an unforeseen problem has occurred and give the author a chance to explain the obstacle and provide a solution for overcoming it, which is especially useful in interim reports or revision plans. Here's a typical example of a funding agency's reporting guidelines (from the Andrew W. Mellon Foundation) that requires a description of activities during the project:

- a summary of the project and purpose of the grant;
- progress made toward the expected outcomes of the grant [project] and any other significant accomplishments;
- any setbacks or challenges;
- significant board, management, or staff changes;
- plans and goals for the upcoming reporting period or, in the case of the final report, of the period subsequent to the grant.

Discussing setbacks can be tricky. However, it's important for the stakeholders to understand whether their work is being completed, and how.

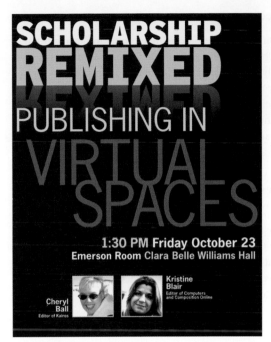

Figure 5.18 A Flyer Advertising a Speaking Event

Courtesy of Phillip Johnson

So how do you focus on the lessons you learned in a report?

Phillip, a student in one of Jenny's classes, designed the "Scholarship Remixed" flyer in **Figure 5.18** and was required to write a final report for that project. In the excerpt that follows, you can see how Phillip researched the flyer genre, brainstormed by sketching initial ideas, and worked through the criteria for the assignment to consider the rhetorical situation. His report discusses his design and rhetorical choices, and it reflects on his composing process to analyze what worked well and how he might improve both the flyer and his design process in the future.

Preproduction process

I started out thinking about what ideas or images the words might evoke. I gravitated toward the "Scholarship Remixed: Publishing in Virtual Spaces" title because the ideas of remixing and spaces open up lots of possibilities.

I surfed my favorite design sites to look at typefaces and color schemes. I also sketched some drawings to work out the density and hierarchy of the information and to work through a few layout ideas. I decided fairly early on this would be a typographic layout and that I wanted it to be bold in order to stand out from the clutter of a bulletin board.

Rhetorical choices

I suppose the decision to focus on producing a typographic layout is the main rhetorical choice I made. Given that the audience for this presentation is mainly English students, it seemed appropriate to focus on the words and try to find ways to make them interesting without losing readability or clarity. For me, the purpose of a flyer like this is to convince people to show up by focusing on the *what*, along with the *where* and *when*. Toward that end, I made sure that the time and place info is not hidden or ambiguous.

Design principles

Repetition is present in the design and is most apparent in the treatment of the photos and the accompanying text, even though the elements are not exact repeats. Colors also repeat to help unify and balance the design. Alignment is working with the various type elements on a number of levels. Proximity is most obvious in the relationship of the photos to each other and to their accompanying text.

Type

As this was always intended to be a typographic design, I spent a lot of time picking out the typefaces. I used Interstate for the bolder typeface at the top of the design, along with a few variants of News Gothic for everything else. I like the contrast between the two typefaces.

Here are some questions you should consider when reporting on your multimodal project to your stakeholders or clients:

- What were the primary ideas and intentions that guided your project?
- What were the key **rhetorical choices** you made?
- What was your **purpose** in creating this project?
- Who was your intended **audience**, and what did you do to attend to their needs or interests?
- What **context** did you design this project to be used in, and why?
- How did you select the **genre** that you used for your project?
- What were the key **design choices** you made? How did you make use of emphasis, contrast, organization, alignment, and proximity?
- What shaped your decisions about the **arrangement** of elements in your project, whether on paper, on screen, or in video or audio?

- What were your key **modal choices**? Which modes did you use, and why?

- What shaped your **dissemination choices** for how and where you would share your project with your audience?

- What were your most significant **project challenges and successes** as you planned, researched, drafted, and revised your multimodal project?

- What would you do differently if you started over? What lessons did you learn that can be applied to future projects?

write/design! assignment

Reporting on Your Project

Analyze the situation to determine what kind of project report you should create to fulfill your clients' needs. Use the questions in the previous section (or others you and your client or supervisor create) to produce an interim or final report on your multimodal project for your stakeholders.

You might also use other documentation you've created for your project along the way, including the proposal, rough draft summary, style guide, delivery plan, and revision plan. Depending on your client's needs, your final report might include all of the major texts you've produced as part of this project, but it might also need to be short and to the point, pulling together the most relevant information about the project and process for the stakeholders. If you're writing the final report, a key issue to address is where the project itself resides or how it will be delivered—your delivery plan. (To help build out your delivery plan, you might refer to sections in Part Two, especially Preparing for the Multimodal After-life, in Chapter 7, pp. 201–4.)

Here are some additional points to cover in your final report:

- **Overview:** What are the major rhetorical goals of your project? How were they met?

- **Audience:** Who are the target readers/users/viewers of the project, and what design choices have you made to accommodate them?

- **Design:** What ideas guided your organization of this project? If it's a print text, presentation, or webtext, where should key elements be placed? If it's a video, audio, or animation project, what guidelines can you offer for how elements are ordered, compressed, or edited?

- **Media:** What stylistic considerations are there for images, audio, or video used in the project?

If this is an interim report, you should also include a section that describes what's going well or wrong, as well as any additional challenges the project is facing. All of these documents together will help you form a more sustainable documentation guide for your audience, clients, or stakeholders. Once you've finished the final report and the project, make plans to turn these materials over to the appropriate stakeholder—your client, instructor, or a different audience. Unless you and the client have arranged for further upkeep on the project after you've turned it in, you're done. Congratulations!

write/design! option: Reflecting on Your Project

Perhaps you didn't work for a stakeholder other than your instructor. Or, perhaps in addition to the final reporting, your instructor or supervisor wants you to reflect on your learning throughout the design process—this is a great way to show your personal growth as a writer/designer. You can still refer back to and include any previous texts you created for your project, such as a proposal, style guide, or delivery plan. In fact, you may be required to if you're creating a portfolio for your project or course.

In addition, you might be asked to reflect on how the project you created meets the learning goals of the rhetorical situation or course. You might be asked to document why the design, media, and modal choices were important ones to reach your audience and what you learned by doing so. This document should be as long as your supervisor or instructor requires, so make sure you continue to perform those genre and rhetorical analysis skills even on reflection documents. Now that you've been through the whole multimodal composition process, the workflows you used in this book will be helpful regardless of genre and modality. Good luck!

The
Write/Design
Toolkit

Working with Multimodal Assets and Sources

You probably know the term **sources** already, but what are **assets**? *Sources* are texts, such as books, articles, websites, and so on, that you can use to gather information about a topic or genre. Assets are pieces of content you'll actually use in your project. An *asset* might be a quotation, an image, a video clip, or a screenshot. For instance, let's say that for your project you need a twenty-second clip from a two-minute YouTube video. The source is the two-minute video (akin to a book or an article you pull from a shelf or the Web). The twenty-second clip from the video is your asset. You'll gather assets from your sources—and, depending on your project, you might create your own assets (for example, by filming an interview with a friend).

Websites and other digital media are updated frequently, so it's important that you save a copy of any asset you think you may want to use when you first find it. Things on the Web disappear.

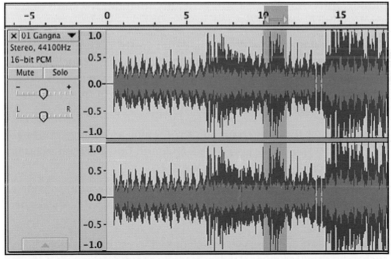

Figure 6.1 A Source and an Asset

In this waveform illustration of an audio clip, the entire song is the **source**, while the grayed-out selection between the ten-second mark and the eleven-and-a-half-second mark is the **asset** that will be used in the project.

For example, Jenny was giving a presentation about online adoption profiles and had planned to show a couple's website while she talked. She did not take a screenshot or save any of the images. Sure enough, the website was taken down the day before her presentation, and she had to scramble to find and analyze a new example. You can save screenshots of websites in an online references manager program like Zotero or in your own filing system (see Chapter 7 for file storage and sharing tips).

Collecting Assets

As you are creating a plan for your multimodal project, whether that's a storyboard, script, mock-up, outline, or other form of pre-writing/designing (see Chapter 7 for more ideas on drafting), you'll want to make sure you create a source and asset list to help you keep your ideas in one place. You are likely familiar with source lists, more commonly referred to as works cited lists or bibliographies. (We'll talk more about those later in another section of this chapter, Citing Assets and Sources, on pp. 160–66.) A well-organized multimodal project also includes an asset list. Asset lists, like the one the Touchpoints in this chapter have you build, help you keep track of the items you are using in your project and can help you think through why you're using those items in the first place. It can also help in creating the final bibliography. An asset list will generally include two kinds of assets: repurposed and created.

Repurposed assets are those you didn't create yourself and are borrowing from other authors (with their permission), such as screenshots, found images, prerecorded sound or movie clips, quotations from written sources, and so on. For the repurposed assets, consider the following questions:

- Where is the asset coming from? Include any source information so you can easily go back later and find the asset again if you need to.

- How will you get the asset from its original location to your project files? What technologies might you need to make that conversion/relocation happen?

Created assets are those you make yourself to use in your project, such as by shooting original video, recording sound, taking photos, writing text, designing logos, and so on. For created assets, consider the following questions that impact your multimodal composition process:

- What hardware (cameras, sound recording equipment, markers, paper) and software (sound or video editing software, photo manipulation programs, etc.) do you need access to in order to create and edit your assets?

- How much time will it take to create these assets for your project? As with any project, especially projects using digital technology, remember that you will almost certainly need some extra time to troubleshoot.

For both types of assets, you should also ask these questions:

- How will any particular asset help you convey the purpose of your project? What is its individual purpose within the larger project context?

- Why are you choosing a particular asset genre or medium over another? (For instance, why choose this sound clip instead of another sound clip? Or, why choose this sound clip instead of an image?)

For example, writer/designer Courteney created an asset list for a video she made to analyze action movies. Most of her video would be comprised of created assets. She decided to break down her created asset column to include both "needs" (the assets and other materials she needs to create for her project) and "solutions" (how she imagines she will get these assets). Working from this table, she made sure her room was ready, asked her actor friends for help in advance, and made sure the camera's battery was charged well before she set out to film anything.

Courteney's Assets Chart

Needs	Solutions
Bedroom setting	Use my bedroom when roommate is in class.
Narrator (actress)	Me; wear motorcycle jacket
Muse (actress)	Sarah, my friend in the theater department
Release form for actress	Get a sample copy from instructor; print out before filming with Sarah.
Video camera	Check this out from the school library (what are its hours?).
Video editing program for PC	I can't use the Mac lab at school because I work during open hours, so I'll use my laptop, which has Movie Maker on it.

Touchpoint: Building an Asset List

If you're not already at work on a multimodal project, imagine you've been asked to create a flyer advertising an event of your choice happening at your college (a sporting event, department lecture, reading series, etc.). These flyers will be put up both on campus and in local community establishments (coffee shops, grocery stores, restaurants, etc.). Make a rough sketch of what you want your flyer to look like so as to help you think through what assets you will need.

Now, create an asset list that will help you gather the items you need to write/ design the flyer. Or, if you're already working on a multimodal assignment, create an asset list for your project. For your list, design two sections: one for created assets, and one for repurposed assets. Make sure each asset has its own row, then create a column for each of the questions listed in the Collecting Assets section (pp. 148–49). Use the questions there to guide you as you fill in your table.

If you are working on a large-scale multimodal project, the Touchpoints throughout this chapter will ask you to return to this list and add to it. To accommodate that work, you may want to create a table that includes assets listed in each row and the summary/descriptions requested as column headers.

Working with Multimodal Sources

Working with multimodal sources and assets often requires strategies for collecting, citing, and sharing that are different from the research processes you may be familiar with. This section will discuss how to find credible sources for your project. As a reminder, sources are texts, such as books, articles, websites, and so on, that you can use to gather information about a topic or genre.

Find Credible Sources

Every kind of text has a point to make and some type of argument it wants to get across, even if it's just to persuade the reader to pay attention to the information presented. For this reason, you need to think strategically about your sources. No matter what type of multimodal project you create—whether it's a promotional flyer, an informational website, a family scrapbook, or an annual report—you should ask yourself what kinds of sources, information, and evidence are going to be the most convincing to the audience you are trying to reach.

In all rhetorical situations, authors need to consider how best to build their credibility so that audiences trust their knowledge and character. This credibility is called *ethos*. Using credible and reliable sources is

Figure 6.2
Credible Sources
Make You Credible

Finding and citing
credible sources will
prevent people from
calling you a dog.

Peter Steiner/The New Yorker
Collection/The Cartoon Bank

"On the Internet, nobody knows you're a dog."

one of the most common ways of building ethos, and it is probably a
tactic you've used when writing traditional research papers for which
you were required to draw on scholarly sources, such as books and
journal articles. That kind of source material can be equally useful
in multimodal projects, but you can also build ethos by having a
well-designed project that pays attention to *how* the text works, as
well as *why* it works the way it does, as we discussed in Chapter 3.
And the design comes not only from creating your own multimodal
content but also from finding outside multimodal sources or assets
(such as images, sound clips, Web templates, screenshots, photos, line
drawings, and graphs) that can lend credibility to your project. (And
for the record, scholars also produce "scholarly" texts beyond books
and journal articles, such as the webtexts used in many examples
throughout this book.)

Evaluate Sources

The following are some questions that you might use to evaluate
whether your potential multimodal sources are credible. Some of
the questions may be more important than others for your project. Remember that the credibility of sources will depend on your
answers to the kinds of questions we have listed (so make sure you
can answer those questions in relation to each choice) and *also* on
the rhetorical situation and genre of the text you are producing.

- **How do you define credibility in relation to your project goals?** What makes a source credible can differ from project to project. For many projects, for example, a source is made more credible by having a known author. However, if you were composing a project about the human impacts of natural disaster, the inclusion of film or video footage shot by an unknown author in an affected area could prove to be highly persuasive to your target audience. The credibility of a particular source depends on your argument and the rhetorical situation for your text.

- **What is the purpose of your source? Does it seem biased in any way?** Is the purpose of the source to persuade? Does it seem evenhanded? Is it limited to one point of view? If so, should this affect your use of the source? Sometimes it might even strengthen your argument to use sources that are overtly biased, especially if your point is to illustrate how people with different perspectives think or act on a particular issue.

- **What information can you find about the text's creator and/or publisher?** Are the author's or organization's qualifications listed? If not, are they well known? Your audience's familiarity with or preconceptions about the author of a source can influence their response to your argument. For example, a video clip from a national news outlet like CNN may seem more credible to some audiences than others. How can you account for the bias of your intended audience in selecting sources when you might need to persuade them of something they don't already agree with?

- **Have you seen this author or organization referred to in any of your other sources?** A source that is quoted or referenced frequently by other sources is generally one that authors and audiences find useful, whether it's to highlight their credibility and lend evidence to a topic or to critique the original author and purpose.

- **Is the information believable?** Why or why not? Consider also what type of person might find the information unbelievable. For example, if you need a source that explains the Second Amendment, a video that was made by a gunshop owner will have a much different impact on audiences than a video made by a constitutional lawyer.

- **What medium is the source?** Researchers have found that visual evidence (like photos or videos) makes information more believable to audiences, but some audiences may question whether a visual is undoctored. Consider which media will be most credible for your project.

- **Are your sources diverse and inclusive?** Sometimes authors overlook diversity when considering sources, and this can affect the credibility of their text with audiences. Considering diversity and difference reminds us to analyze our audiences and to remember that we always have something new to learn from others. Make sure you aren't interviewing only your friends for an oral history project or choosing to represent only one gender or one race in a project that requires discussion of multiple cultures. Don't try to speak for a population that can speak for itself.

⊚— Touchpoint: **Annotating Credible Sources in an Asset List**

If you are in the process of writing/designing a multimodal project for class, create a list in which you annotate each source you intend to use for your project. If you are not in that process or that stage, choose a recent assignment from any class and create a list in which you annotate each source you used. Where possible, the list should include the following elements:

- **The source's metadata.** Document enough information about the site—including author, title, publication venue, and Web address, if relevant—so that you, your collaborators, or your instructor can go back and find the source.

- **A summary of the source.** Describe the source's medium and give a brief description of the source's content. For example, if you're using a website about Cuban Do-It-Yourself (DIY) practices as a source to understand how different cultures engage with technology, you might describe how the website uses persuasive modes and media to make that point.

- **A description of the asset and its metadata from that source.** For example, if you want to use an image from the Cuban DIY website, you'll want to describe the asset briefly: What kind of image is it? What is it about? Who is its author (if different from the whole site)? What is its Web address, filename, and/or title?

- **A description of how the source or asset relates to your project,** including any important/major issues it discusses that you can use to support your project idea or any important/major issues the source or asset leaves out that your project covers.

Copyright Issues and Ethics

As you search for credible sources and rhetorically appropriate assets for your project, be aware of some ethical issues associated with collecting assets that don't belong to you. The majority of ethical issues we'll address in this section relate to copyright law; those issues include the fair-use principle, obtaining permissions, and the use of copyrighted material that authors have purposely given others more freedom to use under certain Creative Commons designations. While avoiding legal trouble is certainly a good reason to pay attention to copyright issues, it is also just good practice to honor the work of the writers/designers who came before you and composed the texts you are now repurposing.

Copyright

Copyright is a legal device that gives the creator of a text the right to control how that text can be used. For a work to be copyrighted, the United States Copyright Office demands that it meet the following criteria:

1. **Originality.** The work must be an original creation—though it's not really as simple as that because a work that is an adaptation or a transformation of a previous work can be copyrighted.

2. **Fixity.** The work must be capable of being stored in some way. An unrecorded speech cannot be copyrighted; once the speech is written down or videotaped, however, it can be copyrighted.

3. **Minimal creativity.** This category is subjective, but for the most part anything that includes some original work will be eligible for copyright protection. Very short works such as your name, phone numbers, and recipes can't be copyrighted, however, because the amount of creativity required to formulate any of those types of texts is considered to be too minimal. In other words, under copyright law "creativity" is considered to take some effort. How *much* effort is often a matter for lawyers and judges to decide.

The point of copyright is to give an author control over how his or her text is used. Authors are the only ones who can legally distribute and/or sell their work—in short, they are the only ones who should be able to profit from it. The moment an author "fixes" an original idea into a text, he or she immediately has copyright over that text, unless the author signs the rights over to another person or to a group such as a publishing company.

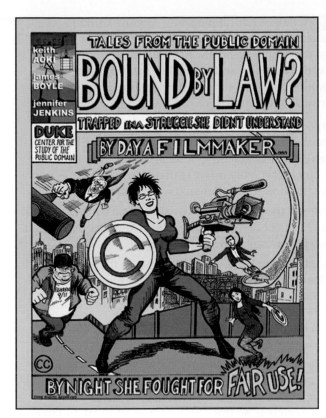

Figure 6.3 *Tales from the Public Domain*

Some works—usually very old ones—aren't covered by copyright. These fall into what's known as the public domain. For more information on public domain, read the comic *Bound by Law?* at http://law.duke.edu/cspd/comics/.

Courtesy of James Boyle

When you're composing a multimodal project, copyright needs to be a prime consideration. As you'll learn in the next section, some of your assets may fall under the guidelines for fair use, but if you ever plan to share your project, make sure that you observe general copyright principles. Sometimes it's easy to forget about copyright because of how simple it is to find images or songs through a quick Web search. But just because you find a source online doesn't mean that it is copyright-free.

Fair Use

Having to consider copyright law for your multimodal project may feel as though your creativity is being limited, but you need to remember that copyright exists in large part to protect an author's original work—and you are probably quite protective of your own work. However, while copyright does exist to protect original authors, the fair-use doctrine limits an author's total control.

The principle of fair use was established to allow authors to use portions of other authors' texts without permission for educational, nonprofit, reportorial, or critical purposes. Anyone working on a multimodal project should pay attention to the rules of fair use. Unfortunately, those rules aren't always clear-cut. But keep the following four criteria in mind, and remember that your usage of the copyrighted work should meet these criteria as stringently as possible in order to qualify as fair use:

1. **The purpose of use.** Is the work being used for nonprofit or educational purposes? Is it being used for criticism, commentary, news reporting, teaching, scholarship, or research? Fair use looks more favorably on texts that meet these criteria and that have transformed the original work into a new use.

2. **The nature of the copyrighted work.** Is it factual? Has it been published? Fair use favors factual published works over unpublished works or forms of artistic expression.

3. **The amount of the work used.** The smaller the portion of the original text you use, the more likely this use is to be protected as fair use, unless you borrow the "heart" of the work, the feature or element that makes the original recognizable. (Although the opposite is true for parodies that require borrowing from and building on the heart of the work.)

4. **The market effect of the use.** Will your re-use affect the market value or sales of the original text? Work excerpted for educational or scholarly purposes often doesn't affect the market value of the original, so this question is good to ask in tandem with the others in this list.

Ariel, one of Kristin's students, was working on a rhetorical analysis of a Web comic for class. She created a website for her analysis that included images, links, and written analysis of the various comics. Because she used screenshots from the Web comics—including different panels from the comics themselves and the mastheads from each comic—she had to think about copyright. Ariel was pretty certain her screenshots fell under fair use for several reasons:

1. The texts would be used for educational purposes—specifically, for criticism and analysis (**purpose of use**).

2. The comics themselves had already been published (**nature of copyrighted work**).

3. She was only using one image out of the entire catalog of comics each author had on his or her site (**small proportion of the whole**).

4. The text would primarily be available only to other people in her class (**small market effect of use**).

Figure 6.4 A Page from Ariel's Webtext Illustrating Her Use of Comic Screenshots

Courtesy of Ariel Popp

While it is often the case that most of your work for class will fall under fair use given the criteria we've discussed, it is important to think through how you are using your sources and assets so that you protect yourself from any legal trouble, as well as honor the writer/designers of the texts you incorporate.

Permissions

In many cases, if you want to use part of a copyrighted text in your own multimodal project, you are supposed to request permission from the copyright owner. In some cases, this might be as simple as sending an email or a letter to a friendly author, who will grant you written permission to use the text for your project. For instance, even though Ariel's plans for using screenshots of the various Web comics safely met the fair-use criteria for copyright, she also expected to eventually use her webtext in her job portfolio, so she needed permission from the authors to use screenshots of their comics and an image of each comic's logo or masthead. The authors wrote back and granted her permission, and Ariel was able to move ahead with her project without fear of violating copyright law.

On the other hand, getting permission from some copyright holders can be overly complicated, expensive, and potentially unnecessary (depending on whether your use of the material is fair). For instance, Courteney, an author who was composing a video-based analysis of action films and who wanted to cite scenes from *The Dark Knight* and other Hollywood movies in her project (see p. 149), discovered that she would have to fill out a lengthy permission form supplied by the films' production company, Warner Brothers, and include a proposal explaining her use of each clip from each Warner Brothers movie. In addition, Courteney would not have been able to use or edit any clips from these movies without first getting approval and (most likely) paying a fee.

Most DIY multimodal projects (like the kind we discuss in this book) don't have a budget, so the actions of requesting permission and paying for the use of clips can raise more ethical and economic issues than they solve. That's when we encourage you to exercise your fair-use rights, transforming an asset for your project by critiquing or studying it for academic purposes, parodying it (among other appropriate fair uses), or using more permissions-friendly clips from a Creative Commons or similar search (discussed in the next section).

When Humans Are the Text

You may need a different kind of permission if you are interviewing a person about his or her personal attitudes, beliefs, experiences, and the like. Most organizations (institutions of higher learning, in particular) require you to have your project approved by the local institutional review board (IRB) if the project involves research that experiments on people or asks personal questions of people, *and* if you plan on making the project public. IRBs exist to make sure that certain research—in this case, human subjects research—is conducted ethically.

For a film that she planned to show only in class (a use that is *not* considered public), Courteney needed another kind of permission: the permission of the actor she wanted to film. She could have requested a signed consent form from the actor or obtained vocal permission recorded on film. If people are recognizable in your footage, you need their permission.

Creative Commons

Confused or frustrated about copyright, fair use, and permissions? Look into Creative Commons, a nonprofit organization devoted to giving authors more control over how their work is used. Creative Commons (CC) also provides researchers with a massive collection of assets that are easily searchable and that can be used without worrying about strict copyright laws, ensuring fair use, or asking (and paying) for permissions. Authors can choose from six licenses, each of which is some combination of the following:

Attribution (BY): Users may copy, distribute, display, and perform the work and make derivative works based on it only if they give the author or licensor credit in the manner specified by the license.

No Derivative Works (ND): Users may copy, distribute, display, and perform only verbatim copies of the work, not derivative works based on it.

Noncommercial (NC): Users may copy, distribute, display, and perform the work and make derivative works based on it only for noncommercial purposes.

ShareAlike (SA): Users may distribute derivative works only under a license identical to the license that governs the original work.

Creative Commons. Made available by Creative Commons Attribution 4.0 International license.

A text licensed with an Attribution-Noncommercial (BY-NC) license can be used in your non-commercial project as long as you give the original author credit. The other great thing about Creative Commons is that you can license your own work after you've completed your project. (If you use any CC assets with the ShareAlike designation, you *must* apply a Creative Commons ShareAlike license to your project.)

When creating your project, you'll want to think about

- What kind of license might work best for you. Remember, if you don't apply a CC license to your work, it will automatically fall under copyright protection.

- What your stakeholders want. Discuss with stakeholders which kind of license your project might need. If your project is primarily for your classmates and teacher, consider how and why a CC license might be helpful. Make a note of which license would be best for your project and why.

Figure 6.5 The Formation of Creative Commons

CC's signature animated film covers the basics of why it formed, what it does, and how it works. Watch the video at https://creativecommons .org/about/videos/get-creative/.

Creative Commons. Made available by Creative Commons Attribution 4.0 International license.

 Touchpoint: Tracking Copyright and CC-Licensed Work

Use an asset list you have created for your project, or return to the asset list you started in the Annotating Credible Sources in an Asset List Touchpoint on page 153. If you haven't completed that Touchpoint, take the time to do so now.

Next, add a "Rights" column to your table. The column should designate one of the following choices for each asset:

- **Get permission:** The asset is copyrighted, and thus its use requires permission. Include information for where and how to do that.

- **Fair use:** Refer directly to the four fair-use criteria and indicate how your use of the asset qualifies as fair. Rhetorical analysis is a good method for indicating this use.

- **CC-licensed:** Indicate which CC license this asset has and what uses the license allows.

For any assets you have that do not fall under fair use, try searching the Creative Commons-licensed assets at http://search.creativecommons.org/ to find additional sources that might replace those copyrighted assets. Remember to look for assets that can be used commercially or can be modified, if these needs are relevant to your multimodal project. Also consider creating your own original assets instead of using those of others.

Citing Assets and Sources

Strict citation rules such as those of the Modern Language Association (MLA) and the American Psychological Association (APA) often are difficult to use when you're producing multimodal projects. This is because those guides were created primarily for print-based scholarship, such as essays, articles, and class papers. You *might* use MLA, APA, or some other citation style in your multimodal project, but that will depend entirely on your genre and rhetorical situation.

In this book, we have only two rules for citations:

1. Provide enough information about each source so that readers can find it themselves.
2. Use a citation style that is credible within the context of the genre you've chosen to produce.

Why these two rules? Because attributing your sources shows that you care about your readers, your text, and the authors whose work you're using, which helps readers interpret and even sympathize with your argument—not to mention that it helps with your credibility.

Different style guides call your source list different things. You are likely already familiar, as a student, with the type of source list called a bibliography. The MLA style guide calls the same type of source list a works cited list. The APA style guide calls it a references list. A film or other media project would call it credits. What you call your list of citations (if you even have or need a list of all the citations in your project) will depend on what genre your project is.

Figure 6.6 How to Cite a Cereal Box in MLA Style

Martine Courant Rife created a video about citing a cereal box in MLA format. As Rife says, "If you can cite a cereal box, you can cite anything." Citation styles can be quite malleable for anyone encountering multimedia genres.

Provide Enough Information for Readers

It's infuriating when someone you trust shares a link to an image (say, a lolcat) on Facebook or via email without including any additional context, and the link turns out to be "404 Not Found"—that is, a dead end. In that situation, you might ask your friend for more information (if you cared enough to follow up), launch an image search of the entire Internet for the correct lolcat (if you don't know which website it appeared on), and then sort through the 427,000 hits to find an image that you *think* is the one your friend sent you. To avoid creating this sort of frustration, you should provide enough information so that readers will be able to find your sources or will at least know that you attributed your sources well enough to give credit where credit is due. And they'll like you for that.

Here are a few basic questions to help you credit your sources:

- Where is the source's home?
- What is its address?
- What is its name?
- Who is its owner?
- When was it born?

(Yes, it's sort of like finding the home of a lost puppy.)

LOST DOG

Name
Male/Female
Breed
Coloring
Date last seen
Place last seen
If found, please call owner at
123-456-7890

Figure 6.7 Finding Missing Things

Photo courtesy of Jennifer Sheppard

Let's ask these questions about the screenshot in **Figure 6.8**.

First of all, what is this asset's **home** and **address**? Let's say you ran across this image on Facebook and didn't know what it was, but you had a link you could click on so that you could read it in the context of the original site. You'd follow the link, which is the image's address (http://www.phdcomics.com/comics/archive.php?comicid=405), and from there you could discover the rest of the missing information. The asset's home is the website the comic lives on, called *Piled Higher and Deeper*. Note that the address of a Web asset is usually *not* the same thing as the main page (the main page in this case would be http://www.phdcomics.com/comics.php). For the purpose of citation, a main page is like the street name of a lost puppy's home—close, but not quite enough information to get the cute little thing back to its owners. So make sure you get the specific Web address, not just the main page address.

What is the image's name? In this case, it's the comic's title. In many websites, the title of a text that is part of a collection will be listed at the top of the browser, along with the collection's name. If the title is not listed at the top, study the page to see if you can figure out what the title is. In this image, the name appears in capital letters on the comic itself: "Deciphering Academese."

Now, who owns this cute little thing? On a website that's designed like a blog or Tumblr, the author may not be readily evident, so

Figure 6.8 Piled Higher and Deeper (PhD) by Jorge Cham

"Piled Higher and Deeper" by Jorge Cham, www.phdcomics.com

search for links with words like *About* or *Author*, or look for a copyright note, which is where we find Jorge Cham's name. Cham is the owner of this comic. (Note that when you don't have the author's full name, you can use their Internet handle—for example, s2ceball.)

Finally, on blog-like websites such as this one, each post is usually tagged with the publication date, otherwise known as the birth date. In this case, the publication date is January 18, 2004. Now we have enough information to track down the asset again, if we need to, and we can use the name, owner, birth date, home, and address to create a citation.

Use a Credible Citation Style for Your Genre

This is usually the point in the production cycle where the MLA or APA style guide or *The Chicago Manual of Style* (*CMOS* or Chicago) gets pulled out—or a website that has examples of these citation styles gets pulled up. But for your multimodal project, you can't assume that you'll use MLA, APA, or Chicago style. Instead, you need to consider what citation styles look like *in the genre* that meets your rhetorical needs. Here's an easy example: when you go to the movies, the soundtrack credits don't appear in MLA style at the end. Readers have come to expect that the sound citations in a movie will follow the format shown in **Figure 6.9**. When you use this style

Figure 6.9 Music Credits in a Film
DreamWorks/Photofest

in a movie, it makes your citations credible, professional, and easily recognizable by your audience.

Not as common with a general audience but still functioning within its own genre conventions, the DJ Edit Pack also uses its own citation practices. An edit pack is a collection of songs, usually grouped by musical genre (punk, rap, electronic, etc.), that the DJ has altered in some fashion in order to make the track more dance-floor friendly. These edit packs are generally used by other DJs who are looking for new music to play or include in their own mix tapes, though occasionally fans of the DJ will listen to the packs as well. **Figure 6.10** shows a screenshot of Portland-based DJ Doc Adam's Punk Edits Vol. 1 Edit Pack. Notice the format for these citations. Each track includes the original artist, the song title, and the name of the DJ who edited the track (in this case, Doc Adam). While it's quite simple, it's the accepted convention for this genre. The point is that citation options vary as much as the genre and its features do. More likely than not, those citations look nothing like MLA-style citations, for example. So this rule is about knowing your genre and figuring out how readers of that genre expect citations to appear.

Figure 6.10 DJ Doc Adam's Edit Pack

Courtesy of Adam Arola

Touchpoint: Finding and Citing Sources

This screenshot is from a webtext (a scholarly, multimedia article) published in the online journal *Kairos*. Locate the original webtext and create a citation appropriate for the genre of multimodal project you're working on.

Figure 6.11 Find and Cite This Webtext

Courtesy of Melanie Yergeau

You can also apply this practice to the rest of your assets in your multimodal project, using the Assets List you created (or will now create) in the Tracking Copyright and CC-Licensed Work Touchpoint on page 153. Add a "Citations" column to your assets list. This is where you will decide how your assets will be cited in your final project. Look to other texts similar to the multimodal project you're working on and see how they include citation information. Remember our two rules for citations: provide enough information about each source so that readers can find it themselves, and use a citation style that is credible within the context of the genre you've chosen to produce.

Organizing and Sharing Assets

In our digital age, we often put stuff online and then forget about it. We don't have a good plan to archive things, which may be fine for Snapchats and random photos, but if you're working for a client or even doing a class project, you may need to keep copies of your work or ensure that you have continued access to it for years to come. For instance, you might need to create a project portfolio to get a job or woo future clients. So consider where you might keep, and how you might organize, copies of everything you make, in case the hosting site you're using goes bankrupt.

If you're working in a group, or even if you're working alone but across multiple computers in a lab, at work, or at home, you'll need to find a good way to share your multimodal assets. Using a USB flash drive or an external hard drive can work in some cases—except when you lose the drive, forget to bring it with you, drop it, or try to save files on it that are too big. Online cloud storage sites are a great alternative. These sites allow you to register (sometimes for free) and save files remotely on their Internet servers so that you can access the files from any other computer, smartphone, or netbook connected to the Internet. These sites are usually password-protected, so you can back up your private files online (although the sites do come with security risks, so don't upload all your banking information!), and you can share project-based folders with anyone you are collaborating with. Examples of these sites include Dropbox, Google Drive, and Box.

No matter what type of sharing system you use, it's good practice to name and organize your files and folders clearly. Doing so will help you find items and keep track of which assets you've already edited, and it will also help other users collaborate, edit, or revise your project later, whether or not you're available. In this section, you'll find some tips for naming, organizing, and sharing your assets. These tips are specific to certain kinds of media files. For instance, avoiding spaces and punctuation in filenames is useful when producing multimodal projects in certain kinds of technological systems (websites, audio files, etc.) but not as important with other types of systems (presentation software like Prezi or blogging platforms like WordPress). Although following a standard set of guidelines will ensure that your final project will work across all software and media types, you do have some flexibility in managing your assets, depending on the genre, technology, and media you're using or producing.

Categorize Your Files Appropriately

Creating folders will help you keep your assets organized and will help you find them again when you need them, just as keeping your clothes organized in a dresser or on shelves makes it easier to get dressed in the morning. Most effective folder structures are arranged in a hierarchy, with the broadest categories at the top, and with the categories getting progressively more detailed as they go down.

Follow these suggestions for using a folder structure to keep your assets organized:

- **Keep all of your project files in one place.** Some software programs require you to keep the files in a specific location. Research the requirements of your chosen software program and follow its instructions.

- **Create a folder structure** that will be easy to maintain throughout the design and revision process.

  Take a look at the example in **Figure 6.12**. This multimodal book review appeared in the online journal *Kairos*. On the root (or main) folder level are the .html files and then folders for .css files, images, and media. Notice how there are no spaces or capital letters in this file structure and how each folder's name clearly indicates which assets it will include.

- **Name your files and folders** according to what they *are* and what they *do*. If you're using multiple images, sound clips, and videos, you might create three folders called *images*, *sound*, and *video*. (See the discussion of naming conventions in the following section.)

Figure 6.12
File Structure of a Web-Based Book Review

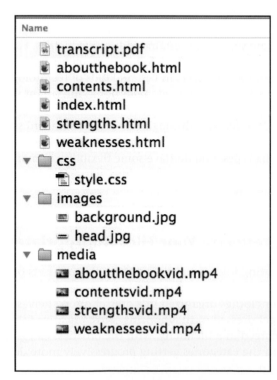

- **Create a separate folder for editable files** that won't go in the final project (we call these *working files*).

Use Good Naming Conventions

Certain types of technologies, such as the Web, rely on exact characters to find files. For example, if you save an .html page as "PuPPies.html," you will find it in a Web browser only by typing the exact filename—that is, *not* "Puppies.html" or "puPPies.html." If you can't remember whether you capitalized the first (or second or third) letter, then you won't be able to find your file. Here are some best practices for naming files:

- **Use all lowercase letters in filenames.** If you know that you use all lowercase letters without exception, then you'll know to (1) name the file "puppies.html" and (2) look for "puppies. html" in your Web browser.

Figure 6.13 Be Careful When Naming Something "Final"

"Piled Higher and Deeper" by Jorge Cham, www.phdcomics.com

- **Use hyphens (-) or underscores (_) instead of spaces.** Web browsers and some multimedia editing programs can't read spaces, and/or they will translate them to a "%20" symbol (which nobody can understand), so it's best to avoid spaces entirely (as in the filename "student-interviews10-11 .mov").

- **Be brief and informative.** Instead of naming an image "red_butterfly_on_fence_in_spring.jpg," consider using "red _butterfly.jpg" as the filename. Or simply call it "butterfly.jpg" if this is your only image of a butterfly.

Use Version Control

You will likely compile multiple versions of your assets throughout your project. For instance, you'll need to crop that audio track from two minutes to ten seconds. If you are exchanging files or using an online, shared repository such as Dropbox, using version control is especially important so that you don't accidentally save over a revised version, causing you to lose new work.

- **If you plan to include dates in your filenames, decide as a group what date format you will use.** Will it be MM_DD_YYYY (for example, "clip1_10_23_2011.mov") or MM_DD_YY? Dates in filenames are OK, but everyone on your team needs to use them in a consistent manner.

- **Use an online version control system.** Git, Subversion, Mercurial, and the like (some are free) automatically assign versions to your project files. Using these can be a little more complicated than just naming a file, but they will ensure that there is no confusion among versions, particularly if you are collaborating on different stages of a project. They also provide cloud-based backups of your work.

⊙— Touchpoint: **Getting Your Assets In Order**

We cannot stress enough the importance of organizing your working files! Without taking proper care to manage your assets and sources, you might start making duplicates or accidentally overwriting your only versions.

Using the sections in this chapter, complete the following checklist to create a clean and rhetorically understandable working environment. Even if you're creating an analog project with analog assets, such as a scrapbook or poster, you can apply these principles through methods such as clearly labeling manila folders for different kinds of assets and working through paper-based mock-ups before using your only color copy of a photograph in your final draft.

- ❏ Categorize your files (pp. 167–69)

- ❏ Apply appropriate filenaming conventions (pp. 169–70)

- ❏ Set up a system for version control (p. 170)

- ❏ Create a system of tracking copyright and sharing assets with your project team or stakeholders (pp. 154–60 and pp. 166–67)

7 Working with Technologies

You have an idea of the *what* and the *how* of your project. You've found sources that can help you get started. Now it's time to think about the practical steps you will take to start building your project. This chapter covers some possibilities for designing multimodal projects and asks you to consider the affordances offered by various analog and digital technologies. (For more on affordances, see Understanding Modes, Media, and Affordances in Chapter 1, pp. 22–27.) In addition to thinking about projects that create brand new content, you can also think about ways of repurposing existing or found artifacts. That is, your project might be a mix of original content created by you, plus content, such as images or video clips found on YouTube, that you integrate and relate to your rhetorical situation. The sections here complement the projects you will create in the Write/Design! activities in Part One. Because your choice of media and technologies will change depending on your rhetorical situation, you might use different parts of this chapter than your classmates use—that's OK! Figure out what makes sense for your project and purpose, then use the information in this chapter that supports your design.

Choosing How to Work with Technologies

When it comes to building a multimodal project, there are hundreds of technology options to choose from. Any number of technologies may work best for your *current* project, but next month you might be working on a completely different project that needs a totally different piece of technology, so we can't just say, "Use WordPress!" or "Learn Movie Maker!" Instead, we offer suggestions for *learning how to learn* which technologies might be most useful for you in any given writing situation. With new technologies emerging every day, as well as constant updates to the applications we already use, learning how to learn about the new affordances and constraints these offer is a critical skill.

People who excel at integrating new approaches and technologies often have the following mindset:

- **An openness to seeking help from a variety of sources.** People who embrace this mindset are generally unafraid to ask questions of experienced users and spend time searching for and using diverse sources of help. These might include print manuals, online tutorials, YouTube videos, conversations with colleagues, discussion forums, tech support via email or chat, and in-application help.

- **A positive attitude toward change.** Rather than dreading the process of learning how to integrate a new process or use a new tool, these people focus on the benefits of their efforts to learn and adapt. They seek out new applications or new versions of older ones to capitalize on improved features.

- **Curiosity.** Rather than making a snap judgement about a new idea or tool, people who use their curiosity to ask questions and to explore possibilities of new features tend to take fuller advantage of new affordances.

- **Vulnerability and a willingness to take risks.** Meaningful learning often takes place when people experiment and try out new possibilities. Often, these early attempts aren't fully successful, but they allow learners to see elements that work, problem areas that need more development, and hypotheses about how to proceed more productively the next time. People with this mindset don't see these attempts as failures but as chances to learn-through-doing.

- **A commitment to problem-solving.** Instead of seeing problems as insurmountable roadblocks, people who think critically and creatively about alternatives are actively learning about approaches that will help them proceed. Some of the best solutions come from trying out new approaches or adapting old ones to fit the new affordances.

◎— Touchpoint: Learning How to Learn

With these strategies and characteristics of successful writer/designers in mind, make a list of your personal approaches to learning new software, applications, or updates. What sites or discussion forums do you rely on? Do you use printed materials and if so, which ones and why? Do you prefer textual, visual, or audio instructions, or some combination? What factors influence your choices and why? What is one new method for learning you could try in your current project?

Deciding Between Analog and Digital

One essential choice in planning your project is whether it should be in analog or digital format. Remember that your multimodal project doesn't have to be digital. Perhaps you'll be delivering your multimodal project on posterboard at a student research showcase or a community meeting, or as a flyer tacked to the office bulletin board or campus event board in the student center. However, even if you're planning to deliver your project on paper or in person, you may still need to gather digital assets and use digital technologies to produce it; for example, you may want to use InDesign to create a printed brochure, or Canva to design a flyer for bulletin boards across your campus.

But what if you were to choose both? **Figure 7.1** shows a slide from a student team's digital PowerPoint presentation on the Chicano Park Memorial Murals in San Diego, California. **Figure 7.2** shows a print/analog handout the team used to support the message of their on-screen presentation. It contains a photo and short description of each mural they discussed in their presentation. This is an example of a project team choosing both analog and digital texts for their rhetorical situation.

Figure 7.1 Presentation Slide

Figure 7.2 Presentation Handout

Courtesy of Alejandra Villavicienco, Joyce Melendez, Alicia Leon, Sarah Tanori

What Does Your Audience Need?

Not all of the questions listed here will apply to your project, but they might help you think through the entire production process—from idea to use—in more concrete terms so that your project planning won't encounter too many surprises or obstacles. The questions here are meant to prompt ideas.

- Who are the primary users or audience members of your project? What are they like? How can you research to find out more information about them?

- What modes and media should you use to reach them? Do you have any restrictions on the technical or media forms of your project? (For example, are you required to make a flyer, app, podcast?)

- Where will your audience get access to your project? What is the viewing context? Will your audience look at a print or analog copy of your project, an online version, or an electronic file stored in the cloud or on an external drive? If your project has digital components, you may need to research the file-size limitations of online hosting sites. If your project is analog, consider its physical size (or weight) and how it will be used in the location in which it's made and where it will be used—for example, how will you get it one from location to another?

- Should access to your project be restricted to your audience or client, or should it be available to people who may not be part of your intended audience? When you upload a video to YouTube, for example, you can set it to be viewable by any user or restrict access to just the people you share the link with. Are you allowed to share, based on permissions or confidentiality issues?

- Will your audience need any special hardware or software to view/use your project? For example, if you created a webtext in HTML/CSS, any Web browser will be able to display the files. But if you design for a desktop platform, your project might not render properly on a mobile phone. How will you make sure that your audience has the right technical setup? For analog projects, such as a poster presentation, how will it be attached to a display stand or wall? Which area of a room or building will provide the best viewing area for your audience, given traffic patterns and possible crowds? And who provides the stand? The tape? What kind of tape do you need to secure it properly?

- Is your project platform-dependent? Some programs export file types that are viewable only on a single platform, such as a Mac or PC. How will your audience gain access to the platform they need to view your project? Or can you create the project in multiple file types? What file format should you save your project in so that your audience can most easily access it?

For example, if you've created an audio project, have you exported your final version as an MP3 so that it can be played on a wide variety of computers and devices? If you want to supplement your digital files with analog accompaniments, will there be a place to display printouts, flyers, or brochures so that your audience will be sure to see them? If your project needs to be printed, have you provided the printer with the correct file type?

- What resolution or compression quality should you use given the final project genre and medium? If you are producing materials for print, their resolution should be a minimum of 300 PPI (pixels per inch). If you're creating a video that you want to be viewable on the Web, you'll need to carefully balance image quality with file size so that users can start to watch the video as quickly as possible but still see clear images.

The choice of media and technology is highly dependent on the primary audience's needs within the rhetorical situation of your project. These questions are meant to help you make these choices with your project team early in the hands-on design process so that you will have a successful transition from the proposal stage to rough cut and rough draft. We go in-depth with some of the technology choices in the next section, Assessing Technological Affordances (pp. 177–81), so read ahead if you want to consider project type in relation to technological affordances before doing the Touchpoint activity that follows.

◉— Touchpoint: **Choosing an Analog or Digital Project**

Imagine you're planning your own multimedia presentation with an accompanying handout for members of the audience. Brainstorm a pitch or plan for the presentation components, considering questions like the following:

- What is the subject and purpose of the presentation?

- What information should go in the presentation, and what should go in the handout?

- For the presentation component, what technologies will you use? What assets will you include? You'll probably want to choose a technology designed for this purpose, such as PowerPoint or Prezi. You may cut and paste text from a word-processing application and may need to use other programs like Photoshop or iMovie to edit images or video to embed in your slides.

- For the handout component, how will you design it so that the message and tone are consistent with your rhetorical situation and the content of your presentation? Would a hand-drawn representation of your content be appropriate for your audience and purpose? Should you use a word processor to create a straightforward and polished text-only document, or could an infographic, made with a site like Piktochart, help you to create a more condensed and engaging communication?

The best way to make a decision about whether you should create an analog or digital project is to keep in mind your audience and purpose while also thinking about your access to and ability with various technologies.

Assessing Technological Affordances

Choosing a technology for your project will depend on many factors, including your project's rhetorical situation, the modes and media you need to suit that situation, and the affordances of the technologies available to you to design with those rhetorical needs in mind. When choosing a technology, take a bit of time to explore what is available to you, what you know how to do, and what skills you can learn or software you can acquire given your budget and project timeline.

The short list that follows identifies technologies that can be used to create or edit different media. The list includes some of the most commonly used applications, but plenty of other software is available, and more is developed all the time. (This list may become outdated, as technologies change rapidly, but searching for some of these programs might help you find other, more up-to-date ones.) Additionally, since mobile devices and tablets have begun offering more robust media capturing and editing capabilities, there is a large and ever-growing selection of mobile multimodal authoring/editing apps. A quick brainstorm with your project team or classmates will produce a robust list for each mobile platform type.

Some of these programs have affordances that allow you to produce multiple kinds of media objects, so our list based on media type (video, website, etc.) is somewhat fluid. The Touchpoint at the end of this section, Conducting a Technology Review (pp. 180–81), asks you to research what some of those affordances are in relation to your project. In the meantime, consider the following example of one student's research process to assess which technologies she would use in her project.

Technology Choices for Multimodal Authoring

I need to design . . .	I can use . . .
Video	Windows Movie Maker, Apple iMovie, Final Cut Pro, Media Composer, Adobe Premiere, Sony Vegas, YouTube Editor
Audio	Audacity, GarageBand, Twisted Wave, WavePad, Logic Pro, Pro Tools
Images	GIMP, Adobe Photoshop, Adobe Illustrator, CorelDRAW, Microsoft Paint, Canva, Fotor, Pixlr Editor, Paint.NET
Infographics	Piktochart, Venngage, Visme, Easel.ly
Website	Adobe Dreamweaver, KompoZer, Nvu, Squarespace, Wix, Scalar, text editors such as BBEdit, TextWrangler, NotePad, Atom
Blog	Blogger, WordPress, Weebly, Moveable Type, TypePad, Tumblr
Pages/Posters	Microsoft Publisher, Adobe InDesign, most word-processing programs, Canva, construction paper, stencils, printer, scissors, ruler, etc.
Animation	Blender, Comic Life, Adobe Animate, Synfig, Xtranormal
Presentation/Slide Show	Microsoft PowerPoint, Apple Keynote, Prezi, Google Slides
Screen Captures	Snapz Pro X, Camtasia, Snagit, Screencast-O-Matic, Jing, Quicktime, TinyTake
Micro- and Multimedia Blogs	Tumblr, Twitter, Storify, Pinterest

In one of Kristin's classes, students were asked to compose a genre analysis website. One student, Ariel, knew she wanted to compose a Web-based comic, but she wasn't sure which Web editor would be the best choice. Ariel had never done any Web design before, so she had to carefully think through what would work best given her project, her timeline, and her learning style.

Ariel knew she wanted to create a very simple website so that the comic itself would be the visual focus on the page. Someone reading a print-based comic can usually see many panels at once, but Ariel felt that her comic would be more effective if the user could see only one panel at a time. Because of this, she decided her Web page needed to have a slide show embedded in it. She also

Figure 7.3 Free CSS Template

Ariel used this free HTML template from http://www. freecsstemplates.org/preview/throughout. Ariel's final version of her site deleted the bottom section of the template.

Courtesy of freecsstemplates.org. Made available by Creative Commons 3.0 license

wanted to learn a bit more about coding in HTML, but she was hesitant to code from scratch since she had never done it before and had only a limited amount of time in which to get the project done. Given that she wanted a simple Web page with an embedded slide show and was willing to play around with code, she decided to search for a free HTML template that she could modify.

Ariel downloaded a template from freecsstemplates.org (see **Fig. 7.3**) and began playing with the code, using the basics that Kristin provided and tutorials she found online. She edited the colors and headers to her liking and then inserted her comic into the slide show. Ariel knew a little about HTML and was willing to learn a bit more, but she wasn't confident about starting from scratch; thus the template was the best choice for her. While she was worried about the template looking a bit bland, the design of the comic itself gave her site visual interest.

Choosing an image editor for drawing her comics was significantly easier. Ariel knew she wanted a crude, hand-drawn look similar to the one found in *Hyperbole and a Half*, a webcomic she analyzed for her project. Microsoft Paint, the program used by Allie Brosh to draw *Hyperbole and a Half*, would achieve the rhetorical effect Ariel was looking for and was easy for her to use, and she already had it on her home computer.

Figure 7.4 A Panel from Ariel's Comic, Drawn in Microsoft Paint

Courtesy of Ariel Popp

◉— Touchpoint: **Conducting a Technology Review**

Review the Technology Choices for Multimodal Authoring chart on page 178 and choose a set of programs that you think might be the best match for your project's needs. (Depending on your project, you may need several different kinds of programs, such as a photo editor, an audio editor, and a Web editor.) If you are not currently at work on a multimodal project, use this exercise to explore a program you're curious about or would like to use in a future project. If you are writing an essay, use this exercise to practice thinking about techno-logical affordances in programs such as Microsoft Word.

Create a chart for each technology or program you want to explore. In the left column of each chart, list the questions below.

- What does this tool do? What is its purpose? (Is it an HTML editor, a sound editor, a social media application, or something else?) What kinds of texts are usually made using this technology?

- Is the tool platform-specific (Mac/PC/Linux) or is it only available online?

- Do you have access to this software? Do you already own a copy, is it installed on computers in labs you have access to, or is it available as a free download or on a trial basis for a long-enough period of time for you to complete your project?

- How does the program work? (This is not meant to be a huge tutorial; just note the basic compositional or editorial features.)

- How steep is the learning curve, and will you have the time and resources to learn enough about the technology to complete your project? What are some tutorial sites or videos that seem effective for learning the basics?

- What do you need to do before you can start designing in the technology? (Do you collect assets elsewhere and import them into the program, or do you "record" directly into it?) Do you need additional technologies, like an external video camera or audio recorder, to make this tool function the way it's supposed to?

- What are the benefits of using this particular technology for the genre of your multimodal project? What are the drawbacks? What does the technology do or not do that will affect how you compose a text in your chosen genre? What file formats does it import and export?

As you research a particular technology, jot down your answer to each question in the right column of the corresponding chart. Compare your answers about the different technologies to help you choose the technology that will best suit your needs. If none are suitable, pick another subset of programs and begin your research process again. Then, based on the affordances you've listed in your chart, choose which program (or set) you will explore further to complete your multimodal project.

Drafting Your Project: Static, Dynamic, and Timeline-Based Texts

As we've discussed throughout *Writer/Designer*, your rhetorical situation shapes your project and the variety of forms it might take. Not only will each final product look different and be used in different ways, but the form and function of each draft will also differ. For example, if you are creating a *static* text like a poster or a flyer, your drafting process might produce some quick sketches, followed by more detailed mock-ups of design plans, and conclude with a polished version printed on glossy paper. In contrast, if you are planning a *dynamic* website for your project, you might begin with some notes on what elements you want the interface to include, followed by a paper-based sketch of the site's layout and navigation, followed by a wireframe to specify the visual details like width and image placement. The drafting process might then culminate in a rough but functional version of your site that you can use to get feedback from your audience and to test for usability. (You can learn more about all of these types of drafts later in this section.)

No matter what mode you are working in or what kind of draft you create, these initial versions of a text allow writer/designers to work through some of the trickier aspects of a project for themselves, as well as to show more concrete drafts to audiences or stakeholders for feedback. In this chapter, we highlight the drafting process and products for three different categories of texts you might produce.

Static texts are those that are set or fixed once an author has completed the writing/designing process. For example, once you finish a written essay or a menu, the content itself doesn't change when the audience interacts with it. They simply read through it in a linear way. Drafts for static texts include rapid prototypes, outlines, models, and some mock-ups. In contrast, **dynamic interactive texts** are those where the audience has choices about which parts of the content they read or interact with at any given time, and the text doesn't advance without the ongoing choices of the reader. The best example is a website where users choose the order of the text based on the links they select. As a writer/designer, you have to consider not only your overall message but also how the parts will fit together when read in any order. Drafts for dynamic interactive texts include wireframes and mock-ups. Finally, a **timeline-based text** is one the audience experiences in a linear sequence such as a film, video, or podcast. As the author, you arrange segments of content (audio, video, written text, etc.) to lead your audience along a path, building your message or argument with each element you weave in. Drafts for timeline-based texts include storyboards, scripts, and rough cuts.

While all drafts are used to bring ideas to life in a physical form, each draft also takes a form that is appropriate to the genre in which you are working. Some of the drafting activities in the following sections can apply across this spectrum of text types, while others, like storyboards, are appropriate for only certain kinds of texts. In this chapter we discuss these drafting activities in relation to the kinds of texts that generally use them. But keep in mind, you can adapt these draft stages or combine them in ways that best fit the medium or genre you are creating.

Prototyping for Static Texts

Product designers create drafts of their static projects that are sometimes called **prototypes** (see **Fig. 7.5**). The term *prototype* can be used broadly to mean "draft" in a variety of forms, but it is often used to refer to a draft that is functional or visual enough to present to reviewers or stakeholders, giving them a clear idea of how the final project will work or look. Prototypes also allow writer/designers to see what their project would look like in a physical form before it is complete so that it can be tested.

Figure 7.5 Rapid Prototyping in Action with a 3D Printer

The printer adds gingerbread to this model of a medieval church.

Courtesy of William Kempton

To avoid spending time, money, and energy on final products that don't work, designers often use a process called *rapid prototyping*. Tom Kelly, creative director at the design consultancy company IDEO, is well known for developing his company's motto: "fail often, succeed sooner." This mantra, now widely adopted in all kinds of business and industry, encourages quick and continual refinement of new ideas based on analysis of what did and didn't work in previous versions. That is, rather than spending weeks, months, or even years perfecting a design that may then soon be obsolete or otherwise doesn't work, rapid prototyping encourages writer/designers to draft and test small changes on a fast and perpetual basis. This has the advantages of shorter development times; creating features that are more fitting for target audiences; and, ultimately, designing texts that successfully fit the rhetorical situation. Rapid prototypes are becoming increasingly common as the availability of 3D printers becomes more widespread (check with your campus library, instructional technology center, or entrepreneurship organization to see if there is one you can use locally).

While 3D printer models are often associated with rapid prototyping processes, there are many other draft types that would also work during this stage of the design process. Draft types for static multimodal projects, such as outlines, sketches, and models, can all be used to solicit quick and repeated feedback from users and to make design changes as a result.

Outlines

One of the easiest ways to get started drafting any kind of project is to make an **outline**, which lists main points, followed by supporting points and evidence. Outlines may be formal, using roman numerals and letters to designate hierarchies (I, ii, A, b), or they may

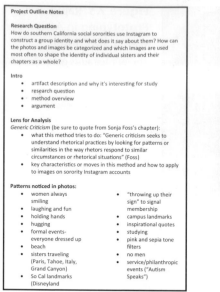

Figure 7.6 The Student's Outline

Courtesy of Jennifer Sheppard

Figure 7.7 The Student's Final Essay

Courtesy of Jennifer Sheppard

be simplified, using indents and bullets. By starting to map out the general organization and structure of your plan, you can begin to visualize what kinds of assets you'll need to gather (textual research, images, video clips, etc.) and how you can arrange them to lead your audience through your argument or message.

In **Figure 7.6**, one student created a basic outline to plan the content and structure of her project, which analyzed how sororities at her university construct their identities through the photos they post to Instagram. One of her points focused on sisterhood and how pictures of sorority sisters holding hands the student shape this identity. The outline helped the student organize her ideas, so when she wrote her final essay, she integrated images from various sorority Instagram feeds as visual evidence for her analysis, including pictures of sisters holding hands, which you can see in **Figure 7.7**. While the final essay's organization changed a little from her original outline, starting with that drafting document laid out a clear map for the student to approach the writing/designing of her project.

Sketches

One of the best ways to begin transforming your static project ideas into concrete designs is to sketch them on paper. Almost any type of text can benefit from producing **sketches**, and sketching your

Figure 7.8 Sample Sketch
Courtesy of Hannah Willis

Figure 7.9 Revised Mock-Up
Courtesy of Hannah Willis

initial ideas has a number of advantages. First, you can quickly generate a number of options without having to wrangle with software. Second, because you have spent little time on these sketches, you are likely to be more receptive to tweaks or major overhauls based on feedback from peers or stakeholders. In the sample sketch (**Fig. 7.8**) and revised mock-up (**Fig. 7.9**), several small but important refinements, such as dropping the second row of horizontal navigation and incorporating the orange color, resulted from suggestions during a peer review session of the initial sketch. Remember, making beautiful sketches is not the point, so don't worry if you don't have the skills of an artist. You are trying to visualize your possibilities here and to work out some initial challenges before you spend too much time going down a path that dead-ends.

Models

Models are drafts for static texts, and they help writer/designers see what their project would look like in physical form, often in miniature, before it is completed. Models are important because they offer a concrete representation of a project so that design and development plans can be reviewed and revised *before* major time and resources are invested.

Architects, who are designers of 3D buildings (a type of multimodal text), call their drafts models. Architectural models can come in a range of completeness, as you can see in **Figure 7.10** (p. 186).

Architectural models work by juxtaposing the relationship of the new (the wooden part) with the existing (the white cardboard or plastic part). This kind of example is good to think about if you only need to customize *part* of a project. Sometimes drafts can be *very* drafty, as in this model, which shows the two rooftop additions simply as shapes positioned in wood.

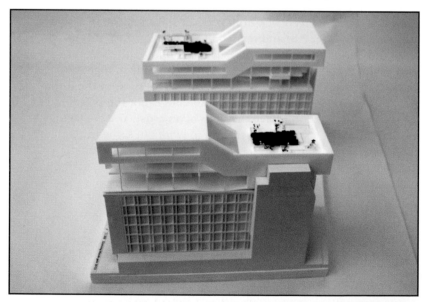

Models for new designs might be crafted in stages. Here is a more complete rendering of the two rooftop additions for a new office/living space with roof gardens on an existing building.

Figure 7.10 Architectural Models

Courtesy of Gro Krüger, Marte Guldvik, and Ole Fredrik Kleivene

Touchpoint: Sketching a Draft

Begin an outline, rough sketch, or model of what your current project might look like. Or, if you're not currently working on a project, do some initial sketches for an invitation you might design for your next party or event. Don't worry if your drawing skills aren't sophisticated. The point here is to generate ideas quickly and explore possibilities about which elements to include and how to arrange them, not to create a final product.

1. Refer back to your rhetorical situation and make a list of the most import-ant features you need to include. Keep in mind that while your design is important in setting your project's tone and helping your readers navigate through it, your most important task is to communicate your message.

2. Once you have a rough sketch you are satisfied with, create two or three more, trying to make them as different as possible from the first. Many designers refer to these small, quick sketches as **thumbnails**, and they use them to rough out their initial ideas.

By forcing yourself to come up with several different approaches, you'll work through the pros and cons of several possibilities and may find, in later itera-tions, that combining elements from different designs best meets your needs.

Designing Drafts of Dynamic Texts

Creating drafts of dynamic texts, such as websites and pop-up books, requires that you attend to a project's naviga-tional features. You might use static drafting techniques like outlining and sketching to get you part of the way in your design, but dynamic drafting techniques like making wireframes and mock-ups allow you to really map out the action of your interactive project.

Wireframes

Wireframes are used for dynamic, interactive texts in that they are created to be blueprints or skeletal outlines for how a project will be organized. They are most often used in planning websites: in addi-tion to arranging content, they also specify important components of the site's interface and navigation and how those will look and function across each page within the site.

In **Figure 7.11**, the designer of a website for family nutrition has specified the placement of several elements on the page: navigation

Figure 7.11 A
Wireframe for a
Website

Courtesy of Edreanne Calaycay

cues and icons, sections for specific audiences such as parents and children, and footer content that will be available on every page. Wireframes are an important part of the development process for websites because they offer a quick way to assess usability and how the layout of a site can support or hinder users' access to information.

You can use online tools that were created for speed sketching of interface layouts, such as Balsamiq, which features pre-made navigation icons and templates that can be dragged and dropped with ease, allowing writer/designers to map layout ideas quickly without worrying too much about aesthetics or the coding necessary to create a website.

Mock-Ups

A **mock-up** is a rough layout of a screen or page. Mock-ups differ from sketches (see pp. 184–85) because they are typically used further along in the development process, after you have decided on which sketched idea you want to pursue. They are commonly used for drafting any type of static composition that is primarily visual, such as a poster, an album cover, or a brochure. They are also used frequently in the design of dynamic, interactive texts like websites because they provide a visual snapshot of a site's basic layout and design.

Essentially, a mock-up is a visual outline of a project. A good mock-up should include the proposed layout, colors, images, fonts, and recurring elements such as headers. Though mock-ups may include the actual textual content, often they do not. The idea is to create a kind of road map that shows where everything will eventually go, not to actually create the finished product. Web authors often compose

Figure 7.12 Tapiola Veterinary Hospital Website Mock-Up
This mock-up shows where the main content on each page of this site will be as well as how the navigation will work within the drop-down menus.

Courtesy of Kristin Arola

Figure 7.13 A Mock-Up Design for The Kitchen Sync
Courtesy of Nick Winters

mock-ups by hand, on paper, or in some type of screen-based software such as Photoshop. You can also create mock-ups using word processors, spreadsheets, or slideshow software. It's not so much *how* you create the mock-up that's important as *what* the mock-up illustrates.

Figure 7.13 shows a professional Web design mock-up for The Kitchen Sync, a boutique kitchen supply store located in Wenatchee, Washington. The clients (the owners of the store) wanted a website that provided a professional boutique feel while also showcasing the different products the store had to offer. The main goal was to get people to visit the physical store itself. While the clients had some ideas about what they wanted the site to look like, the Web designer wanted to show them a rough layout with a few different color and image options. Notice that on the left-hand side of this mock-up you see possible colors, textures, and images. On the right-hand side, you see possible headings and buttons.

As writer/designers, we often find that our first ideas about how to arrange elements need tweaking once we start visualizing them on paper, and they sometimes don't work at all. By first sketching out really rough layouts or wireframes and then revising and making changes in our mock-ups, we ultimately save ourselves time and create more successful designs.

◎— **Touchpoint: Drafting Your Wireframe and Mock-Up**

If you are designing a wireframe or mock-up for your multimodal project—or if you are a classmate or stakeholder reviewing another writer/designer's draft—use the following checklist to consider questions or evaluate the design.

❏ Is the proposed layout evident? Is it consistent across all possible iterations (pages) of the text? If the layout needs to change to indicate different sections or areas of a text, are those variations indicated in separate or supplementary mock-ups?

❏ Is the color scheme clearly indicated? Is it appropriate for the rhetorical situation and for readability?

❏ If images are used, is their relative placement on the page or screen mock-up purposeful and consistent across all versions?

❏ Are example fonts provided, and if so, do they adequately reflect the rhetorical needs of the text (e.g., did you use display type for headlines and body type for larger amounts of written content)?

❏ Are the navigational elements shown or indicated? Are they clear for users? Are they consistent across all iterations?

Composing Timeline-Based Drafts

Timeline-based drafts are used for any type of project that includes a chronological progression that audiences will watch, read, or hear. If you are creating a video, audio text, or a timed slideshow, for example, the drafting methods we discuss in this section—storyboards, scripts, and rough cuts—might be what you need.

Storyboards

A **storyboard** is a sequence of drawings, much like a comic book or visual outline, that represents the movement, spatial arrangement, and soundtracks of objects or characters in shots, screens, or scenes.

Because they illustrate elements in a sequence, storyboards work best for timeline-based projects, such as videos, audio pieces, or animations.

A storyboard represents a text that moves through time, such as a video, visual podcast, or an animation. Like mock-ups, storyboards may include rough visuals, but they use visuals to show the sequence of the project, as well as written descriptions of the actions or sound effects that need to take place at each moment. Storyboards can be incredibly complex but a simple storyboard consisting only of stick figures and a few arrows to show directionality can also be surprisingly effective. As with mock-ups, the important thing is not how artistic the storyboards are but that they indicate what elements (setting, script, images, soundtrack, or effects) and actions (movement, lighting, camera angle, etc.) need to occur at which point.

The goal of an effective storyboard, no matter its level of complexity, is to capture as much information as possible and help you decide what shots you'll need to film, what audio you'll need to record, or what images you'll need to capture *before* the filming, recording, or animating begins. (See Chapter 6 for more on collecting and organizing assets.) Good planning now will save you

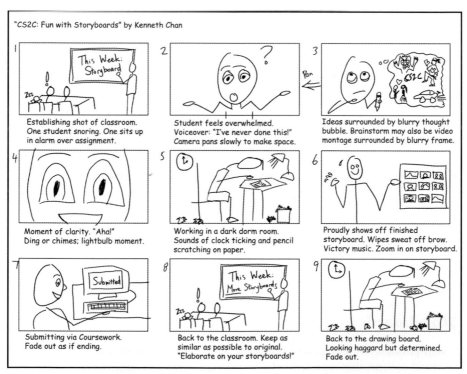

Figure 7.14 **A Storyboard About Making Storyboards**

Courtesy of Kenneth Chan

lots of time and frustration later on, so it's worth the effort. Similar to a mock-up, a storyboard can also help you get feedback on your basic design so that you can adjust it if it isn't working for your audience.

When creating your storyboard, you'll want to think about including notes on the following elements:

- Setting
- Movement by characters or objects

Figure 7.15 The First Six Panels of Courteney's Storyboard

These panels show her introduction of the topic (Panel 1), the beginning of her narrative-based analysis (Panels 2–3, in Courteney's bedroom), and the main characters in the analysis (Panels 4–6, Courteney and her "muse").

Courtesy of Courteney Dowd

- Script/dialogue
- Soundtrack or sound effects
- Shooting angle

Of course, depending on the genre of your project, you may want to make notes on other elements as well.

For instance, Courteney was creating a three-minute video-based analysis on effective action films and had sixty-four panels in her storyboard. **Figure 7.15** (p. 193) is a small segment of Courteney's entire storyboard. You can see that you don't need to be an amazing artist to compose an effective storyboard; you just need to include enough detail so that your audience, teammates, or instructor can figure out what you intend to do and give you feedback on it, and so that you have an outline to work with once you start capturing content.

Figure 7.16 Courteney's Drawing of Herself in Bed (Panel 2 of 64)

Courtesy of Courteney Dowd

Figure 7.17 Courteney's Video of That Scene

Courtesy of Courteney Dowd

Scripts

If your multimodal project will include audio or video, you may need to create a **script**. A script is a draft for a timeline-based project that allows you to specify linguistic content (what will actually get said or shown) and other multimodal elements such as sound effects, visual effects or transitions, stage directions, and more. If you've created a storyboard for your project, writing a script is the next step in putting those ideas into action. As shown in **Figure 7.18**, a script typically includes dialogue, with clear identification of who will say what and when. It will also include details about *how* that content will be presented, such as sound effects, lighting, or the tone of an actor/narrator, and will place them within a timeline to see how all the pieces fit together. A script for a video project will likely include even more detail about what visuals will appear on screen and how they will align with other multimodal content, like music or dialogue.

Writing a script in advance of recording—even if there is no voiceover or dialogue—is useful for accessibility purposes. You can turn your draft script into a transcript to upload with the media files you prepare. That way, readers with different vision, hearing, or neurological accessibility levels can still engage with your project. Plus, making your project accessible to all users is the law in many countries and when creating content for government agencies.

Your script is a detailed roadmap for turning your storyboards into a working project, but keep in mind that you'll likely have to make adjustments as you begin filming/recording.

Client: Whitman County

Job Title: 30sec Radio Commercial

Commercial Title: Your Opinion Matters!

MUSIC: (INSTUMENTAL OF THE STAR SPANGLED BANNER)

WOMAN: (FRUSTRATED) Are you tired of all the promises our community makes towards making our community better and safer, but in the end they just never get around to actually fulfilling these promises?

MAN: (ANGRY) Yes, but I wish that during the GOP meeting my opinion would actually be heard on the matter!

WOMAN: (CURIOUS) Well have you ever actually attended a GOP meeting in Whitman County?

MAN: (ASHAMED) Well... No

WOMAN: (EAGER) You should! If you were to attend the next Whitman County GOP meeting, then your opinion would be heard and we could put an end to all of these empty promises. Plus, I heard there is free pizza at every meeting!

MUSIC: (INSTUMENTAL OF THE STAR SPANGLED BANNER OUT)

Figure 7.18 A Script for a Radio Commercial

Kristin Arola

Rough Cuts

Rough cuts are another step in composing timeline-based projects. Using all of the work you've done in previous parts of the drafting process (sketches, storyboards, wireframes), rough cuts are your first attempts at actually building your project and putting the pieces into sequence. Rough cuts are usually missing significant elements such as background soundtracks (with audio or video projects), titles and transitions (audio and video projects), navigation (websites), permanent graphics (posters), and so on.

In addition, rough cuts shouldn't include tightly edited assets, because feedback on your rough cut might indicate that you need to revise your project in a different direction. If you've cut your video down to a ten-second clip, and then reviewers tell you they'd like to see a little more of it, you're out of luck. You want to have enough content left in your assets to be able to add different shots or material to your revised project if your reviewers suggest such changes.

Figure 7.19 A Sample Rough Cut

This rough cut of a video bonnie lenore kyburz is making has all the static photos and animated screen captures in their correct place in the video project timeline (see the bottom half). The sources are also included in the upper left-hand corner. She also still needs to add titles and some transitions between the visuals, but this version of the video is appropriate for a rough cut review, which viewers can watch in the preview window (in the upper right-hand corner).

Courtesy of bonnie lenore kyburz

◉— Touchpoint: **Drafting Your Storyboard**

For most timeline-based texts, a storyboard will be necessary. If you are designing a timeline-based text for your multimodal project—or if you are a classmate or stakeholder reviewing another writer/designer's draft—use the following checklist to consider questions or evaluate the design.

❏ Is the initial setting or context clearly evident? How is each setting or segment change represented auditorially, visually, spatially, or linguistically—via titles, transitions, or other means?

❏ Is each character/interview/subject matter differentiated in some way (if it's necessary to do so)?

❏ Are important character or object movements indicated? (For example, if it's important that a character is seen rolling his or her eyes, have you used arrows around the eyeballs or something else to indicate that movement? Or if a car is supposed to exit the right side of the frame, how have you shown that?)

❏ Are snippets of major dialogue included underneath the storyboard visuals? If not, what are the key ideas that need to be expressed in each scene or segment?

❏ Are sound effects or musical scores noted (usually under the dialogue or scene)? Do you indicate what these audio elements will be and how long or loud they will be?

Getting Feedback on Your Rough Drafts

After you have a draft completed, it's a good time to invoke the feedback loop, particularly from your peers. We discuss peer review in more detail in Chapter 5 in reference to your final drafts (see Peer Reviewing Multimodal Projects, pp. 124–27), but before you get that far, you might also want to present your mock-up, wireframe, storyboard, or rough cut to your instructor or other stakeholders. The presentation of this rough draft may be formal (presenting to a client) or informal (conferencing with a teacher or workshopping with classmates), depending on your writing situation.

Here are some tips for presenting your in-progress rough draft to stakeholders:

- Be able to say why you've made your design choices—for example, you might explain that you chose the color scheme and navigation system for your website mock-up to match the interests of the site's intended audience, or that the nontraditional sequence of your storyboard's scenes is crucial to your text's purpose. At the same time, be open to the comments and suggestions of those you share these early designs with. Sometimes writer/designers get so immersed in their work that they lose a bit of perspective. Keep in mind that feedback from others can help you improve and build on your ideas by tailoring them to the needs of the stakeholders and the rhetorical situation.

- Prepare a list of questions you'd like to ask your reviewers. Refer to checklists in *Writer/Designer* like the Mock-Ups and Storyboards sections (pp. 189–94) to determine the areas that you might want your reviewers to focus on. If you're submitting a rough cut, ask your reviewers to make sure nothing sticks out as odd, out of place, inaudible, or nonsensical. Remember, this is just a rough version of your project. The roughly edited assets should tell enough of the story or argument for your feedback loop to catch what (if anything) doesn't belong and what still may need to be added. (Refer back to Chapter 5, Finalizing Drafts for Your Primary Audience on pp. 119–23, for more on the feedback loop and peer review.)

- Research the genre requirements for your project and provide reviewers with a genre checklist (if appropriate) as they review your documents. (Refer back to Chapter 3 for more on genre.)

- If your stakeholders or colleagues offer feedback, assess that feedback for its usefulness in relation to your project's rhetorical situation, and revise your draft accordingly. (Refer back to Chapter 5, Revising Your Multimodal Project on pp. 134–36, for more on revision plans.)

Preserving Your Assets with Metadata

Deciding on a delivery medium and drafting your multimodal project only fulfills part of the requirements for finalizing all of your hard work. Let's say your delivery medium is the Web, or more specifically a third-party hosting site such as Facebook, YouTube, Prezi, SoundCloud, or Wikimedia. You could just upload your project and walk away. (Although you should tell your client where your project is located!) Maybe you've created a radio essay that you will turn in for a class project, but you also will upload it to a radio-essay website such as StoryCorps. So your teacher is your client, but the website listeners are your audience. How will your intended audience actually *find* your project? How will other people know what it is? How will a computer, which can only scan text, search for your audio file? Metadata is the answer. **Metadata** is data about data: information about a piece of content that can tell a reader who created the content, what it represents, when it was recorded, and other bits of information that make your project findable and usable by others.

Figure 7.20 StoryCorps Web Page with Metadata

The Web page for this Studs Terkel story contains metadata in the form of a title, a recording location, credits, a description, and other data.

You've probably seen keywords, tags, categories, and other metadata on media-sharing sites like Wikimedia Commons. Each media element that an author uploads to Wikimedia Commons has to include written information or data *about* the media element so that Wikimedia can help other users find that element. Without this metadata, the media element won't be easily found by, say, a user searching for the perfect audio sound effect of rain falling in Glenshaw, Pennsylvania, to include in her documentary about that tiny town.

A screenshot of the summary section of the Wikimedia Commons page for the sound effect of "Heavy rain in Glenshaw, PA" (**Fig. 7.21**) shows some of the metadata for this one file. The metadata includes a description of the sound effect, the date it was recorded, the source of the work, the author who created it, what the file's permissions are, where the file was recorded, and a bunch of other information further down the page. Researchers can search for the town name (if they need a specific geographic location), date (if they need a specific time period), and so on from either a search engine or from the Wikimedia Commons home page, where

Figure 7.21 Finding Metadata on a Wikimedia Commons Page

users can browse for content by topic, media type, author, copyright license, or publication source (among other options). All of this information is metadata that the file's author included when he or she uploaded the file to the Web. Additionally, supporting written material such as transcripts of audio/video files and descriptions from proposals can function as metadata for your final project. Including all of this information will help make sure that your project is sustainable.

Preparing for the Multimodal Afterlife

Once you've finished your multimodal project, consider what will happen once you walk away from it. Unless you've set up a *Mission: Impossible*–style self-destruct option (warn your clients if you do), your text will continue to have a life of its own long after you've forgotten about it. This can be good, bad, or worse.

- **Good:** Maybe the "lolcats meowing 'Happy New Year'" video you posted to a video-sharing site goes viral, and you and your cats get invited to appear on a late-night TV show. (Well, that could be a bad thing, too.)

- **Bad:** The photo album of you dancing at a New Year's Eve party, which you unthinkingly posted to your public Facebook account to share with your friends, shows up in a Web search by the human resources department for a company where you recently interviewed for a job that you really need. And they don't hire you.

- **Worse:** You already work for the company and they fire you because somebody in the background of one of those Facebook photos was doing something not just stupid or silly but illegal, and you're now a party to that illegality.

These examples relate primarily to **privacy** issues that all digital media authors need to consider, but authors must also consider **security** issues for the afterlife of their text. In this age of metadata, face-recognition tagging, hackers, and spam, everyone should consider privacy and security. Even Cheryl, a supposed expert in digital media, had her server hacked—during finals week, no less, with all of her syllabi and course assignments on the server—because she hadn't bothered to keep up with the security updates to the blogging software she had installed months or, in some cases, years ago. Getting hacked is just one example of a major security breach that can take days or weeks to fix, if it can even be fixed at all without deleting everything and starting over. And once you're done with a project (particularly if it's for a client or class, and only if you really *don't* need to work on it anymore), the last thing you want to worry about is starting over. So ask yourself the questions in the sections that follow.

Where Are Your Project Files Located?

You may have asked some of these questions in earlier sections when you were beginning to work on your project (such as What Does Your Audience Need?, pp. 174–77), but it's important to refer to this list of questions at multiple points during the write/design process and after your work is completed to ensure privacy, security, and stability for your project.

- If they're stored online, is that online location private (password-protected and/or only available to a limited group of collaborators or clients)?
  - Who do you want to continue having access to that private location? Remove/unshare/delete any users that should no longer have access.
  - Is the location secure enough to leave the files there as a backup?
  - What will you do if that backup location stops providing the service you're using? How often will you check back to see whether the service may be discontinued? Can you set up an automatic notification?
- Is that online location public (available on the Web for any search engine to scan or a potential boss to see)?
  - Do you need to have that final draft available publicly? If not, pull it down. If you do, perhaps you're not really done with this project, and you need to make plans (regarding financial or labor resources, time management, and other things outside the scope of this book's discussion) for maintaining it.
  - Does the metadata for the project allow a level of privacy that you're comfortable with now and will be comfortable with into the future? Will you be able to update the metadata to reflect your changing privacy needs as you get older?

How Long Are You Responsible for the Project?

- How often do you need to check in to that location to make sure your privacy is being maintained?

- How often do you need to perform any upgrades or updates to the location to ensure your privacy and security? Can you set up an automatic update or arrange to be notified automatically when updates need to be made?

- Should you copy online files (whether public or private) to an offline location and delete the online versions?

- Do you need to keep a copy of the files at all?

- If so, what kind of storage device will you keep them on, and how will you ensure that you will be able to use that storage device five years from now? (Remember floppy disks? Zip disks? Probably not . . .) What is your plan for transferring your files to an upgraded storage device, or do you anticipate a time when you will stop caring about the files altogether?

Many of these questions depend on what the project is, how important it is that you and other people continue to have access to it, and what its longevity (its usefulness and rhetorical purposefulness) is expected to be. We're not all famous people who need our every digital file archived in the Library of Congress, but that doesn't mean we should just randomly delete stuff. Depending on your career path, you might need to create a portfolio of your work or refer back to an example or use an old photo in a new project. Be judicious about deleting—it should be a decision that is directly tied to the rhetorical situation of your text, as well as to future, unknown rhetorical situations that are probable, given who you are and what you're likely to do with your life. Storage is cheap and getting cheaper all the time. Plus, you'll never know what you'll want to show your great-grandkids, nieces and nephews, parole officers, or cyborg pets in the future.

Figure 7.22 Keeping Content on Facebook

Should you rely on platforms like Facebook, YouTube, and others to keep your valuable multimedia content safe? No. Always keep backups.

Courtesy of Cheryl Ball. Photos by Xuxa Rodriguez.

Touchpoint: Creating a Sustainability Plan

Use the questions in this chapter to craft a sustainability plan for your project or the work you have done in your class so far this semester. This plan should include descriptions of where the project will reside (i.e., the storage and/ or delivery medium), who will have access to it, what the access codes are (if any), and any other information relevant to the transfer of your project to your client. In other words, how will your project endure after you've completed it? For most of these questions, there is no clear-cut answer. Instead, it is a matter of weighing the pros and cons to find the solution that is best for your project's particular rhetorical situation.

Index